Tell it to Bartender Bob

by Andy Book

©Copyright 2011 by Andy Book

All rights reserved

Published by Reimann Books

December 2011

1st edition

ISBN 000-000-0000

Printed in the U.S.A.

A note from the publisher:

Because of the unique original design of the manuscript with hand drawn illustrations and unique typesetting we felt it better to present Tell it to Bartender Bob in its original manuscript form in order to stay true to the intentions of what the author wanted it to be. We feel that this adds to the style of the book, and we hope that it enhances the reading experience.

IN APPRECIATION

Thanks to Ernie, Guy, Andy, Jack, Joe, Pete, Earl, James, Jason, Frd, Steve, Charlie, Walt, George, Thelma, Gert, Mike, Huey, Ian, Sylvia, Ed, Marty, Kevin, Brian, Leroy, Daisy, Sam, Homer, Jim, Ralph, Len, Harry, Don, Howie, Nat, Tom for their stories.

Also thanks to Aunt Mary and my parents for their help and support.

Evan Book AKA Bartender Bob

Prologue

Life has its problems; seeming insurmountable at times, so many people try to solve them by going to clergy, psychologists, family members, friends and others'

These all have merit, but accompanying drawbacks as you know,. The best one on whom to unload your woes may be the bartender because.....

He listens, doesn't pass judgment, offers you a drink to irrigate your problems and you leave refreshed and ready to battle the saber-tooth tiger once more. Give everyone thine ear and few thy voice is his motto and like Spinosa he doesn't ridicule or condemn but tries to understand. There's nothing good or Bad, thinking makes it so believes Bob

The following are true stories heard by Bartender Bob in the more than thirty years he has been listening- not like a teacher with one year of experience thirty times.

Names have been changed but the narratives are authentic. I'm sure you can probably identify with some episodes even more poignantly. Tell them to Bartender Bob and if he includes them in his next book you get a fat tip and a drink on the house.

tellittobartenderbob.@gmail.com

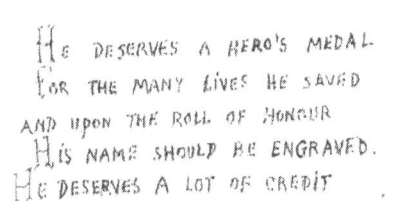

"THE MAN BEHIND THE BAR"

He deserves a hero's medal
For the many lives he saved
And upon the roll of honour
His name should be engraved.
He deserves a lot of credit
For the way he stands the strain;
For the yarns he has to swallow, would drive most of us insane.

He must pay the highest license, he must pay the highest rent,
He must battle with his bank and pay their ten per-cent.
And when it comes to paying bills, he's always on the spot,
He pays for what he sells, whether you pay him or not.

And when you walk into his bar, he'll greet you with a smile,
Be you a worker dressed in overalls or a banker dressed in style.
If you're Irish, English, Scotch, or Welsh, it doesn't matter what;
He'll treat you like a gentleman — unless you prove you're not.

Yet the clergy in the pulpit, and the preacher in the hall,
Will assure him that the churches are against him one and all.
But when the churches plan to hold a ballot or bazaar,
They start by selling tickets, to the man behind the bar.

When he retires, a job well done, to await six feet of soil.
Discards his coat and apron, no more on earth to toil.
As Saint Peter sees him coming, he will leave those gates ajar,
For he knows he had his hell on earth —
"THE MAN BEHIND THE BAR"

Acclaims for "TELL IT TO BARTENDER BOB":

"An extraordinary debut!"   —Housewife, N.J.

"Evan has written a book so mesmerizing that I devoured it in a single gulp, reading it far into the wee hours. His characters will hold you spellbound. This beautifully written book has it all. What reader can ask for more?

—Plumber, OH

"In 'Tell it to Bartender Bob' Evan has created tales of regret, redemption, of honest emotions of characters haunted by their past. Crafted with language so lovely you have to re-read the passages just to be captivated all over again. This is simply a beautiful book. I can't wait to read the next edition."

—Atomic Scientist, Los Alamos

"First time novelist Evan Book has written a heart-wrenching book by turns of light and dark, literary and suspenseful. A natural for discussion groups is recommended."

—Fifth grade student, NYC

"An auspicious debut novel. This book is a page turner. Wonderfully crafted. I highly recommend it."

Inmate, Sing Sing

"Evan Book writes with great wisdom and compassion about people, family, choices and secrets. A wonderful heart-healing collection."

—Welfare recipient, Detroit

"I'm looking forward to new installments of Evan's endearing chronicles with wistful fondness."

—Subway commuter
Washington, DC

"This unusual collection is exciting, probing, dashing and filled with surprises. The writing is memorable and smart. A keeper!"

—A Pulitzer Prise Winner in literature

"Wry, well crafted and wonderfully twisted stories that are a pleasure to read."

CONTENTS

1. Ernie's secret of success
3. WPA wisdom
4. The wall of fame
5. Rumors
7. The fleet's in
9. On the house
10. Where are you from?
11. The uncertainty of shoes
12. You're fired
13. A thirty year moment
15. Under Paris skies
17. A no to Red Cross
18. A Merry Christmas
19. Poco coolo
21. The best "laid" plans
22. The two glass offer ecab!
23. Here comes the judge
24. The wife, the hula dancer
26. Thelma and poetry to live by
29. Teach me more teacher
32. A black Russian
34. Uranium, the new yellow gold
37. Counterfeiting
38. The Coney Island treatment
41. Tatoos anyone?
42. The bastard of a teacher
43. Out of the closet
45. Jury duty
46. Art for art's sake?
47. A Puerto Rican poem
48. San Gennaro's feast
50. Bad news travels fast
52. From 9 to 90
55. An "a-cute" observation
57. A mass murderer
60. Homer
61. Ephemera
65. A poem in a church
66. Cookie jar
67. Reduced to the lowest common denominator
69. World's oldest profession
71. Intermission
72. Non-paying passenger
74. Kopmashnah
76. Lockup
79. Off her rocker
81. Proverbs
83. La Serenata
87. Redhead
89. Thanksgiving turkey
92. Who does a bartender tell his troubles to?
93. Hold the press
95. Taxi! Taxi!
97. Happy Birthday
98. A Parting Poem
99. Epilogue

Ernie's secret of success

Bob: Here's your drink Ernie.

Ernie: Bottom's up. Bob. Here's to Happy Days! And nights too!

Bob: You're always cheerful Ernie, never a hangdog look. What's you're secret?

Ernie: I don't thirst after money. Y'know, I'm only a gofer at the law office, even tho' I was educated an electrical engineer. I live alone in a furnished room, eat all my meals at a diner and have a few drinks here. My life is simple; no wife, woman, Man or kids to complicate it.

Bob: Still I see you're a favorite with the ladies. How come?

Ernie: Bob, each woman has a lonely spot. And women want to feel important just like Men. I find something to compliment them without sounding phoney. Like for Instance, a pin she is wearing. "That's an unusual pin, I never saw one like it." Or Earrings, something else she's wearing. It always works as an opening gambit.

Bob: Sounds good.

Ernie: You don't need a psychology degree, Bob. Another that works is acknowledging People who work for a living. When the cashier asks me, "Anything else?" I Respond with, One more thing, don't lose that smile." Those last four words disarm Any woman. Nobody wants to be considered a grouch. The next time I walk into there She remembers me. Watch me work this angle on that woman at the end of the bar. She doesn't know me nor I her. Watch!

(Ernie leaves his spot and walks over to the woman. She looks warily at this chubby Middle-aged guy approaching. Words are exchanged. Ernie returns to his previous spot)

Bob: I noticed her bland look when you spoke to her, and the smile that followed. You're right Ernie!

Ernie: There you go! Didn't I tell you?

Bob: I gotta try that routine myself on my customers.

......Footnote: A short time later, while changing a light bulb in the law office, Ernie fell off the ladder. He was taken to the hospital where he died.

He left no kin, will or money. His room held newspaper clippings, Books, and copious writings and nothing else. As a veteran he was buried In Arlington National cemetery. An end to a solitary life.

WPA wisdom

Harry, the ol' curmudgeon, ritually comes in every night and has his usual Beer. He leaves his mongrel dog tied up outside. It's only him and his "love on four legs", "Octogeranium" as he facetiously calls himself. He squirreled enough money working minimal wage jobs to live with a roof over his head and beans in his belly. He seems in relatively good health considering his years. He was telling two young lads at the bar a story about the great depression.

"Boys, I pity you. The depression ahead will be much greater than the one I lived through. Like some guy said," You ain't seen nutting yet!" I remember the WPA making a road where we lived. It was pick and shovel, back breaking labor with little Recompense, not like the heavy machinery they use today. Today you see signs saying MEN WORKING and you only see machines. It was a hot, humid summer day. My Mom gave me a bucket of water and a ladle to take to the men. I never forgot the words of a big black man as he took a swig of water. "Boy," he said, "Always remember this.... When ya got a dollar, ya got a friend." To this day I never forgot those wo One of the lads,

" Harry, it's the same today."

The wall of fame

Bob: John, they tell me you were a prospector.

John: Yeah, I prospected for gold, silver copper, gems, a lot of stuff.

Bob: How'd ya do John?

"Well, I made and lost, just like life, win and lose...It's all behind me now.

Bob: How do you measure your success?

John: The one great success was when my partner Howie and I were in this isolated

Village in the New Mexico hills. You would think you were in some alien place. The people spoke little English but were very hospitable. The family that Howie knew let us bunk in their adobe home. They had two sons and a beautiful sixteen year old daughter that looked like a Playboy centerfold, I'm not kidding. I was in my twenties but hands off, as much as I lusted after her. We spent four days there. It was Easter and the father was the pastor of the church which was adobe with an oil skin rag over the small window. He played a flute as they chanted and sang in Spanish. A Group of worshipers picked a fellow, put him in chains, made him carry a cross and beat him as he made the stations. Boy I was glad they didn't chose me!

Before we left I went to the outhouse. Lo and behold, on the wall in a feminine scrawl my name appeared along with three others. Bob, that was definitely my Greatest success in life!

Bob: If you stayed longer John, I'm sure she wouldn't be able to resist your over-age charms.

John: Bob, you'd say so even if you didn't think so.

Bob: John, you'd think so even if I didn't say so.

- They both laughed.

Rumors

Politics, sex, religion, the three topics bandied about in all bars in America and beyond.
We find a motley group of veterans from WW2 to the present wars in the far East
Drinking beer and exchanging views on the political fiasco the WMD

Willie: "Our illustrious leaders, especially the president, believed that rumor and I sit here
   Today minus a leg and arm because of these assholes. I'm bitter.

John: I don't blame you in the least, Willie, they should never have acted on rumors.
Brings back what I learned in High school English class,"What fools these mortals be!"
What do you say, Len?

Len: You're 100 percent right John. My Mom used to say the same thing."The public is
a fool, they accept anything the government tells them." Let me give you guys a concrete
example of how gullible people are.

Bob:(interrupting)Sounds interesting, Len, go on- tell us.

Len: Years ago during WW2 I was Ships Company in Key West Fla. That's a navy term
for those who work on the base keeping the grounds and buildings in top shape. It's a
Good deal because you stay stateside.

   Well, one day my buddy Rich and I were assigned to sweep out the
Officers quarters, a boring job. Rich, a bright guy with a mischievous streak, always
thinks out of the box and you never know what he's going to say or do. When we finished
we went to the canteen to have a beer. Rich told the few guys there that when he was
sweeping out the hallway he heard the announcement on the radio in th officer's room
saying that the Japanese used a new dry ice gas and instantly froze four Russian divisions
to death. Remember this was the time before TV and cell phones. The rumor he started---

-spread rapidly and soon the whole base was buzzing. Somehow it got back that Rich and I started the rumor. We were called on the carpet by the commanding officer and reprimanded. He said he wouldn't give us a Captain's Mast (the lowest court martial charge because he felt that it was such a ridiculous rumor that it surprised him how many sailors and officers actually believed it. Just do the Maintenance work you are assigned to do he advised us and don't start anymore rumors.

Bob: Good thing for you two he didn't court martial you. That could go on your record.

Len: Yeah, However, the next day Rich and I saw our names on the bulletin board To be shipped out to Shoemaker California and the Pacific theater.

Bob: Coincidence? Hummm. What was the commander's name, Len-Smith?

First name Chicken?

The fleet's in!

The seaport comes alive. The Military Sea Transport is returning from the war zone. Crowds converge on the docks to welcome the returning servicemen and ship's crew spilling down the gangplank like rats abandoning a sinking ship..Forklifts, trucks, cranes, booms, all go to work unloading the containers and gear. Ambulances cars, taxis, and hearses appear on the scene. .Yes, the seaport is alive, except of course, the hearses. The married sailors all head for home. The single ones head for the Nearest bar which will be three deep very soon.

Bob greets the familiar faces;

"Welcome back Jim, Ralph, having the usual?"

Jim   Yeah , a shot and a beer chaser, Bob.

Ralph   Me too Bob.

Bob   How was the trip mates?

Jim   Not bad. Good weather but we ran out of booze on the ship. Ralph drank my after shave lotion.

Ralph   I was desperate. Don't worry Jim, I'll replace it.

Bob   I suppose you two studs will be on the prowl for women as you usually are. Like James Howell way back in 1666 said "One hair of a woman can draw More than a hundred pair of oxen."

Jim   Ha! Funny, Bob, but that's not how we say it in the modern Navy.Tell him Ralph.

Ralph   We say a cunt's hair can pull a locomotive.

Bob   That's crude, dude.Then I assume your plans are to latch onto some bimbos?

Jim   Not this time Bob, we need money to spend on them. This time we'll pick up a -

- gay and roll him. Gays are usually well-heeled and weak.

Bob Need money? I'll spot you. Leave the gays be.

Jim Thanks Bob, we don't want to borrow from you and besides, we hate gays.

    After downing a few more boiler-makers Jim and Ralph bid Bob good night and left the bar in seach of gay prey.

    Three days later..........

The swinging doorsopen. Two sailors enter. Both look the worse for wear. They are Heavily bandaged and one is on crutches. Bob recognizes Jim and Ralph.

Bob What happened to you two? Hit by a locomotive?

Jim Not quite. When we left the bar we picked up this gay or better he picked us up.

    He took us to his lavish apartment loaded with expensive furniture, paintings,

    What have you. When we tried to roll him he said that one thing he enjoyed more

    Than sex with men was beating up sailors. That's the last thing we remembered.

Bob Wow! He certainly did a job on you both!

Ralph We wound up in sick bay. Our ship sails next week and hopefully we'll make it.

    From now on it's the weaker sex and the weaker the better.

Jim (pessimistically) Yeah and with our luck she'll be a lady wrestler who beat the Texas

    Red head for the World's title.

Bob Like the Danes say, Advice after injury is like medicine after death. You

    Should have heeded my counsel.

On the house

Guy: Comes into the bar, sits on an empty stool and calls Bob
"Hey bartender!"

Bob: At your service. What 'll you have?

Guy: First I have a story for you. You got time to listen?

Bob: (genially) Sure, I'm all ears.

Guy: There's this fella, Bill, who died. Being a good man, he went to heaven where he sat on a cloud and played a harp all day long. He soon got bored. He complained to St. Pete.

Bob: He had a good deal (commenting)

Guy: You know St. Pete, what a hard-working guy I was back on earth. I'm bored. Give me something to do to last me forever.. St. Pete thought. Then he hands him a cup, tells him to go back on earth and to gather all the dew from all the clouds. That should last him working forever. Gee thanks, St. Pete, he's Happy with the assignment.

Bob: That's it?

Guy: Oh no, more. It's ten years later, he's back at the Pearly Gates. I'm finished he tells St. Pete. Give me something to do that'll last me forever. St. Peter Thinks. Then hands him a silver spoon and tells him to go back on earth and empty the atlantic Ocean into the Pacific. That should last you forever. Thanks St. Pete you know what a hard working guy I was back on earth. He leaves.

Bob: Well, what's----(getting impatient)

Guy: Twenty years later he's back at the Pearly Gates. St. Pete, I finished the job.

The first only took ten years, this one took twenty- you know what a hard-working guy I am; give me something to do that'll last me forever. Hmmm. mused St. Pete, then he said O.K. go back on earth. Go to the bar on State Street and sit there and wait for the bartender to give you a drink On the house. That should last you forever.

Bob: (laughing) You win. What 'll you have? It's on the house.

* note, This story can be applied to many different situations

Where are you from?

Being a bartender for over thirty years, Bob hears all kinds of accents and Is able to pinpoint regions of origin with great accuracy. One woman who Comes in the bar every Saturday has an accent that Bob can't seem to palce.

She is a woman in her 60's, has black hair with straks of gray. She Walks to the stores downtown not owning a car and is known as "Granny" By the locals.

"Granny," Bob says one day, "I tried but I can't place your accent. Would you Tell me where you're from?

Bob standing by the bar waits to hear the name of a state. Granny looks up Nods slightly and slowly says-

"I'm from the earth. Just like you."

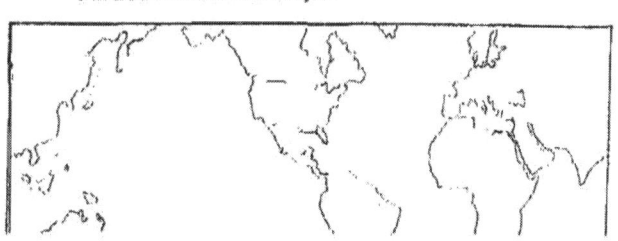

The Uncertaincy of Shoes

Bob: (Greeting an old friend) Well Andy! Been a while. Still doing a Lot of traveling?

Andy: Yeah Bob, nice to be home, seeing the folks. They're not getting Younger y"know nor we but health is the most important, right?

Bob: Righto, Andy!

Andy: Got something I want to share with you. This elderly desk clerk at a Pokemoke Maryland motel I stayed at got to chatting with me about life And she said, "Take care. You go put your shoes on in the morning, you don't know who'll be taking them off your feet at night." sobering thought, Makes carpe diem, seize the day and leave nothing to chance the way to go.

Bob: Lot 'a truth in that.

You're Fired!

Bob: " You look crestfallen, Jack, how did your job hunting turn out?

Jack: (sipping hsi beer) Not too well, Bob. You know that jobs are scarce today.I,ve been on unemployment eight months now. Testerday they sent Me to a warehouse to be a handler, bettern Burger King at least. They outfitted me withglove and steel toes 'cause the job requires heavy lifting. I told the foreman McGinnis that the main office sent me. He took one look at me and said, 'You're fired! Go back to the main office."

Bob: Just like that? Why?

Jack: That's what I asked him. Why? He said, "When a guy comes to work for me with his two hands in his pockets, I know I can't get any work out of him."

Bob: That's the shortest job on record.

Jack: From now on , I report for a job with both hands in full sight, believe me.

A Thirty Year Momemto

Bob: (Remembering) Joe! So how did the get-together go with your old buddy Andy? What was it like 30 years you hadn't seen each other?

Joe: Went great! We talked about old times, us growing up in our factory town. It was probably boring to our wives who were with us. Ah, but there was one incident that perked them up though.

Bob: Which was —? Tell me about it.

Joe: A carnival came to town and me and him snuck under the flap of a tent. Now in those days the religious had censorship over nakedness in exhibitions and-----

Bob: This tent had a nude show

Joe: Yeah, for men only. The place was packed with working class stiffs eager to see naked women. And here came this overly buxom woman, in her 40's completely naked and gyrating her hips around a pole---- Forerunner of what you see now.

Bob: Must've been something.

Joe: Oh, it was exciting no end. We worked our way up to the front of the stage. In our early teens then, sex was still a mystery, not like today with The computer savvy generation. Now you wouldn't believe what Happened.

Bob: What? (Curious)

Joe: Well, Andy reached up and grabbed the crotch of this lady. Startled She looked down to see him. She went and patted his head like he was a little naughty boy and then she pulled out a pubic hair and handed iy To him."Here, Sonny, you can have this when you jerk off." The guys All roared in response!

Bob: How did your wives react to this story?

Joe: They got a charge out of it. But what really floored them when Andy doesn't say a word, grins and opens his wallet. He takes out a small Plastic envelope and--------

Bob: (Laughing) Don't tell me!

Joe: Yeah. Inside was the pubic hair

Under Paris Skies

Bob: So Pete, you being a world traveler, know many tongues, do you speak French?

Pete: (Laughing) Only enough to get my face slapped, Bob. Yeah, I've been in France, Paris as a fact.

Bob: Tell me about it.

Pete: Years ago I was taking a train from Barcelona to Paris. Two girls and Another guy and me shared a four bunk sleeping compartment. We drank wine, ate crackers and cheese and sang along with the guy playing his guitar. He even taught me some French songs on the guitar. We had a great social time, no hanky panky and conked out 'till we arrived in Paris in the morning. We ate breakfast at an outdoor café and then went our individual ways. One of the girls(the prettiest one) gave me her phone number to call and she would show me Paris. I wandered around Paris taking in Some sights and gave her a call at 8 PM. She gave me directions and I took the Metro (very clean no graffiti like NYC) to her pad. Her roommate was Just as beautiful. We talked, drank wine, snacked until 11PM. I thanked them for their hospitality and excused myself to go find a room. In Paris? At this hour? Never. Stay here. You can have the couch. I'll move in with Michelle in the double bed we have. There's a latch on the inside of the Bedroom door. Well I stayed the whole week-end enjoying her hospitality.

She showed me the city and took me to inexpensive restaurants and night clubs. It was time to leave for Rotterdam to pick up a ship back to the U,S. so she saw me off at the railroad station giving me a farewell kiss not to Forget her. To this day I wonder....Did they latch the door?

Bob: The Portuguese say never bolt a door with a boiled carrot. Did you try it at all ?

Pete: No, I was afraid to. There's more. Bob

Bob: Go on.

Pete: Later that year I was planning to go into double harness, get married. My Mom told me there was a call from a girl in New York City .It was her. She got a job with Renault. I gave the phone number and her name to my single friend Frank.He didn't follow up on it. Was that door latched? I'll never know. It haunts me.

Bob: You'll never know, Pete.

A No To Red Cross

Bob: (Having watched patrons give money to a Rd Cross woman who came to the bar) to Earl, who's scowling he asks, What's with you Earl?

Earl: To them I give nothing. The Salvation Army yes. Red Cross gives a salary To Mrs.Dole, over a quarter million bucks for being head leader officers in Salvation Army just get by.

Randy: (Overhears) Well Earl, Bob, I'll tell you 'bout when I was in Okinawa in WW2. The Red Cross canteen showed up. We all ran over for the coffee and doughnuts. Want us to be paying for them—not free like the Salvation Army. And the my horny friend Mario from Brooklyn goes and propositions one of the gilrs. Fifty bucks for a quickie she tells him.

Bob: So what happened?

Randy: What? Yells Mario.He tells her his month's pay including overseas pay is only 60 dollars.The girl counters, the officers pay it.Bet those girls mopped up at army bases.Years later we're selling our blood for 25 dollars a pint to the Hospital. The give us a steak dinner after.We go to sell our blood again and they s Stop buying .Go to the Red Cross. We go and they take donations only. They sell the free blood to the hospital for 75$ a pint. Earl, I'm with you The Salvation Army gets my contribution.

A Merry Christmas

Bob: (Surprised) Hi Jason, I didn't expect to see you tonight. Thought you had a date.

Jason: I did Bob, and with a beauty too, a Vancouver Canadian beauty contest Winner last year. I was really looking forward to taking her out, but it turned out different than I expected.

Bob: Tell me about it Jason.

Jason: I went to her apartment and she's sitting on some suitcases. The place is completely empty. No furniture, TV, nothing. The people she was staying with just up and left. She came back from a trip to find no message or any word.

Bob: You went to your place?

Jason: Well she couldn't move in with me, all I got is a furnished room. So we Got in my car, searched the city, finally found this small efficiency place and I helped her carry her suitycases in. I opened one of them and it surprised me to see that it was filled with only Christmas decorations. And that wasn't all. It seems she carts this suitcase around everywhere. Why? Because, she says, wherever she goes she gotta have Christmas.

Bob: That's some story! So she'll be unpacking tonight and you're here alone. Well, Merry Christmas to you both! (Pouring another drink)

Poco Coolo

Bob: Setting up drinks for two Mexican workers. He listens to bar regular Fred talk with them, " Que hubo ca hombres?" They laugh, "Estamos Jodido, senor, quieremos cervesa "

Bob: Hey Fred, you handle the lingo well.

Fred: Not really but I'm still learning. I gotta tell you this. I got work one time as a social worker in New Mexico. My caseload was about 250. One Recipient lived about 15 miles from town, washboard roads there, drove under 20 miles an hour. I had a 4 cylinder Willis sedan that took all the bumps.

Bob: Pretty isolated, huh?

Fred: The only house there. The woman is sitting on the porch. Lived alone, had some farm animals, a well. It was a cool day so I thought I'd greet her in Spanish. I said to her "Poco cool-o no?" She bristled, "Yes, but not for you, you s.o.b.!" And ran into her house. I stood dumbfounded. After a few minutes, I left.

Bob: (Laughing) Could it be something you said?

Fred: I dunno. The next morning my boss Gus Martinez asked if I interviewed the woman. I told him no and what happened. He called the secretary Maria

Gonzales, told her and they laughed hysterically. I asked why the laughter so Gus explained that what I asked her for was a piece of ass.

Bob: (still laughing) Well, you learned.

Fred: Every morning when I walked into the office everyone greeted me with " Poco Culo, how are you?" standard joke from then on. It's five years later----

Bob: (Enjoying all this) There's more?

Fred: Five years later I called up my former boss who was retired and living in anotther part of the state. His wife answered The phone. she asked who I was. I told her "Culo". And I heard her call out, "Hey Gus, Poco Culo is on the phone!" Since then I got myself "Spanish for Dummies" and followed the proper grammar.

The Best "Laid" Plans

Bob: (Sets up a gin and tonic for Steve entering) How'd ya do last night?

Steve: I was having a great time, Bob. The band was playing sensuos Latin music and I was rubbing bellies with that beautiful brunette all night. She was really turning me on. And when you closed the bar at 3 A.M. she left with me.

Bob: Interesting, go on.

Steve: She gave me directions. I was anxious to connect and was excited thinking she had a pad of her own. When she said to turn left I did to find the road led to a cemetery. She said to drive in. So I thought it'd be a novel experience to do it in a grave yard, at least no one there would complain. When I stopped the car she got out and disappeared

Bob: What did you do then?

Steve: I went to look for her. After wandering through the graves I saw a figure by a grave in a far corner. When I walked over I saw it was her kneeling down crying. There was a picture on the stone of a little boy. It was her illegitimate two year old son who had been killed by a car. When she composed herself, I drove her home.

Bob: (sets anotherGin-and-Tonicfor him and waits for more of the story)

Steve: My desire died in that bone corral, Bob.

Bob: I can understand why. Mine would too.

The Two Glass Offer Eech!

Bob: Welcome back, Charlie! I heard you were in Nashville.

Charlie: Not Nashville, Bob, Newark, New Jersey. Why they've got more Country Western hillbillies there than anyplace. You now I like that music.

Bob: You play it well too. We love hearing you fiddling away.

Charlie: I gotta tell you, the weirdest thing happened there.

Bob: Go on.

Charlie: Well, I walked into this bar on Freulinghausen Avenue. Two whores were sitting there and I engaged them in conversation. They told me that just before I came in ther was a fellow, well dressed, tie and all, salt and pepper hair, rather handsome who came in and sat next to us. He asked us if we would pee in the fluted beer glasses and he would give us five bucks apiece. Well, five bucks is five bucks, so what the hell, we went to the John filled them up and came back to the bar. He gave us the ten bucks, drank both glasses, thanked us and left.

Bob: You believe that?

Charlie: Well, one thing I know about whores, they're honest and of course I believe them. Me? I'll stick to beer. Beer me up, Bob.

Bob: After that story Charlie, you deserve a drink Here you are! Bottoms Up!

Here Comes The Judge!

Bob: Hey, James! I see your friend Chester was appointed judge of the township.

James: He's quite a fellow: you know we grew up together, did a lot of crazy things

Bob: Tell me about them.

James: One was when we were dogging.

Bob: Dogging?

James: That's the expression for spying on parked cars in the lovers' lane area of the woods where we lived We would sneak up on the cars and shine flashlights On the unsuspecting lovers in the back seats. Chet would pick up the discarded Condoms and collect them in a tin can he hid under his front porch.

Bob: Why?

James: When he had a dozen or more, he'd tie them together with string. Then take it to lover's lane. We'd watch while a guy got out of his car to another car for a trst with the girl there. Chet would go to the guy's car and tie the string of condoms all over the license plate obliberating the numbers. We all laughed when the guy returned and drove away with the condoms trailing behind. Imagine the explanation the guy would have to make to his wife once she's seen the license plate and asks him where he's been.

Bob: That's some story James.

James: Well, I hope his kids never hear it. He has eleven you know

The Wife, The Hula Dancer:

Bob: Greetings Walter! How did the PTA variety show go last night? Your wife was in it and I suppose went.

Walt: You didn't hear about it? Pour me a shot and beer chaser.

Bob: No I didn't. Tell me about it.

Walt: To begin, well y'know my wife is active in the PTA. It's a good organization that could improve the school by pressuring the teachers and adminstration to earn their pay. "Shape up or ship out" like we used to say in the Navy. But most of the time they get tied up with politics, raising funds, the meetings, and they get nowhere.

Bob: Yes, that's true. But tell me about last night.

Walt: Yeah well, they had this variety show performances by teachers and PTA members. My wife, Lucy, was in a hula number with four other middle-age mothers.

They made grass skirts and practiced their routine for a few weeks 'till they got it down pat. Lucy looked terrific. She still has a beautiful figure for a woman who had four kids, one after another. It takes a lot of nerve to face an audience of local people, so the girls brought in a bottle of vodka to the teacher's room to fortify themselves before going onstage.

Bob: Well, go on.

Walt: Lucy imbibed way too much. Their number came up, the recorded music began, the five dancers wafted onstage. As they were undulating and moving their hands and arms, Lucy began shedding her grass skirt. And then everything else. Now there were four grass-skirted dancers and one completed naked.

Bob: (Supressing a laugh) Wow.

Walt: Shocked into action, someone threw an overcoat over Lucy and hustled her off the stage. Now how do you top an act like that!

Bob: Probably what followed was deninitely dullsville.

Walt: I'm happy that the schools are closed for the holidays. I hope this blows over before the kids have to return.

Bob: Don't worry Walt, it'll be old news. And in today's paper there's a story from your school having an affair with a student. That'll start tongues wagging on this. Lucy's act is tame compared to this.

Walt: Well I hope so, Bob. Maybe like water and debris under the bridge especially debris.

Bob: Touche!

Thelma and Poetry to Live By:

Bob: (To a patron, Thelma) Say, you're always cheerful. In all the years you've been coming here, you had your share of sorrows, abusive husband, a kid on drugs, going through two divorces and more, yet- what your secret?

Thelma: Well, Bob, my philosophy is Carpe Diem, live for today. Here's a poem that I follow. Care to hear it?

Bob: Yeah. I would.

Thelma: Here goes...

The poet with his pen, the peasant with his plow,
It makes no difference who you are, it's all the same somehow.
The king upon his throne, the jester at his feet,
The shop girl, the actress, the woman on the street.
It's a life of smiles, it's a life of tears,
It's a life of hopes, and a life of fears.
A blinding torrent of rain and a brilliant burst of sun
Biting, tearing pain, and bubbling sparkling fun.
And no matter what you have, don't envy those you meet
It's all the same, it's in the game,
The bitter and the sweet.
If things don't look cheerful, just show a little fight

> For every bit of darkness, there's a little bit of light
> For every bit of hatred, there's a little bit of love
> For every cloudy morning, there's a midnight moon above.

Bob: Beautiful. Who wrote that?
Thelma: Some guy called Anon.
Bob: He wrote a lot of good stuff. I see his name a lot.

Bottoms Up?

Bob: Well, well, well, the three holes in the ground! Look who's back, Millie and Gert! You two haven't graced this joint with your presence in a long time. Where have you two lovely lasses been?

Gert: It's well, well, Bob, there's only two of us. Pour us two beers. We just got back from vacation. To get away from the ice and snow we went to Miami.

Henry: (From an adjacent stool) Gee, it's good to see you both looking so great and sporting nice tans.

Millie: Hiya Henry! Yeah, it was great taking in the beach scene, basking in the sun in our bikinis instead of bundling in our parkas. But it's nice to be back.

Henry: I'll bet those beachcombers got excited seeing your beautiful bodies. I know I would have...pant, pant.

Gert: Henry, you're so horny even a 100 year old woman would excite you.

Henry: Most definitely, Gert. What is it that the Mexicans say, "--anoche todos los gatos son pardos." At night all cats look gray. And Kingfish in the Amos and Andy radio show said, "Women never stop looking, that's why they have shades on a hearse. Anyhow, anything different different with you? Worth talking about besides tanning those beautiful 30-year old hides?

Gert: There's one that a pervert like you would find interesting.

Henry: I represent that remark, Gert, but let's hear it, I'm all ears.

Gert: And all something else, Henry.

Bob: (Interrupting) Enough of the compliments, you two. So tell us about it, Gert.

Gert: Okay. Listen up. Millie and I were enjoying our beers in this hole-in-the-wall...two handsome guys come over and strick up an acquaintance with us. Merry conversation flowed freely. Then drifted, as always into sex. We were getting high, feeling no pain. One of the fellows said he'd give us each $100 to insert one of the beer bottles all the way into our "caverns of joy"..."Snatches" to you Henry.

Henry: And did you?

Gert: That was the easiest C-notes we ever made, right Millie?

Millie: Right, Gert.

Henry: (After what seemed like a profound silence. Hmm... Which end of the bottle did you insert first? (Gert and Millie begin pummeling him as he covers himself from their blows).

Bob: Only you, Henry, could come up with that! Girls, girls that's enough! Here's another rount for you two and Henry. Shall I say, Bottoms Up?

Teach Me More, Teacher:

Mike: Back in '42 Penn Station, New York was an exciting place. Servicemen from all branches of the military hustled to and from trains joined by sweethearts, wives, families saying goodbyes to them on their way off to fight the war.

Bob: Yeah. I was one of them. I can still see myself as I was shipping out.

Mike: I had a two-hour delay there bound for California and my ship. While I was debating what to do for two hours, this pretty brunette came up to me.

Bob: Tell me about it.

Mike: She held a cigarette, I lit it for her. She thanked me as she took a few drag s on it. She asked, "Where are you headed for, sailor?" I told her, Treasure Island, California, I'm assigned to a destroyer, my train doesn't leave for a couple of hours. I asked if she's care for a drink with me. She did. And we headed for the cocktail lounge in the station. We sat close. There was something familiar about her.

Mike: Oh more than that. Much more. Guess what! I strike a match for her cigarette, her face, of course! It's Miss Perks, my Fourth Grade Teacher! And the fragrance the same. It was like I was nine again and she had been helping me at the blackboard with long division and I would never forget her or the scent.

Bob: But did she place you, remember you?

Mike: Actually I must have changed a lot, she didn't seem to recognize me. But, yet, she hadn't aged at all. Or the fragrance. What a stroke of luck meeting her!

Bob: Go on. What happened next? Did you tell her who you were?

Mike: Well, somehow I couldn't, not just then. We left the station together and walked up 8th Avenue and came to a small hotel. I paid the charge. We went into a room. She dressed down to her black bra and panties and slid under the bedsheets. "Honey, how about getting some drinks for us? I like scotch." No problem I said to her. I left to find a liquor store. It was a sailor's dream, booze and a broad in a room.

Bob: So you got the drinks, so you had maybe about an hour together.

Mike: Nope. More. Said to hell with the train. I hurried, got a fifth of pre-war scoth and two six-packs, what luck. But then, of all things, wouldn't you know I run into this couple, Charlie and Irene from high school. They're married, have an apartment close by and work in Manhattan. They wanted me to join them. Charlie, though, made it easy for me, noticing my discom-

Bob: So was she still there in the room?

Mike: Asked me what took me so long. I told her, classmates from Woodbridge High. Undressed down to my skivvies and crawled next to Pauline as I was calling her now. She liked the scotch, smooth it was, she drank it straight. And sang with each good belt. She had this beautiful voice. Sang "La Donna Mobile" and one more aria and another. I made passionate love to her. The bedsprings in rhythm to her singing.

Bob: Must have been some night for you.

Mike: Well we finally drifted off to sleep. I awoke in the morning, she was sleeping peacefully. Beautiful woman. And I never thought I'd become an opera lover.

I left a note for her. In it I wrote, "Your student Mike Maslovsky from fourth grade, you were terrific to me then. And terrific last night. Thanks for the lessons in language and love." I took the next day train, spent time in the brig for being late at my base. But it was all worth it!

Bob: That's some story Mike! Care for a scotch?

Mike: A beer will do fine.

A BLACK RUSSIAN

George: (Comes in, sits at the bar) Well, Bob, we got us a black president. Next thing you know there'll be a drink, the Black American. Like that Black Russian one, vodka, kahlua, right?

Bob: Want me to mix one up for you. (He holds back a grin)

George: No, no. The usual. I got a story for you. Wanna hear it?

Bob: Yeah. Go ahead.

George: It's like family history. I want to tell it right. Okay. It's December, 1913. Four girls, the oldest nineteen, the youngest sixteen. That's my Mom. They are in America after a month at sea. Came through Ellis Island, got on a train and they're at the Perth Amboy train station. Nobody has shown up yet for them. And they see this man coming toward them. He's very dark. Is this a black man that they heard about? They had never seen any black men in their village in Europe.

Bob: That must have been some surprise.

"Добрый День Девочказ!"

George:	Oh yeah. But not like what came next. Well, he stopped, and looked at them, and laughed. Then he shouted out in Russian, "Slava Isusu Christu." the church greeting! They were dumbfounded. But it turned out that he was no more black than they were. In fact, his family the Vrables were from the same village. He was on his way home from work at the coal yard in town, well covered in coal dust. I'll tell you what, that kind and generous man piled them into his truck and drove each one to their new home. He became a life-long family friend. We all called him Yanko.
Bob:	I like that. My parents and uncle and aunt came over from the other side. Young, responsible. Not like the teenagers today.
George:	There's more, if you care to hear it.
Bob:	(Refilling his drink) Go on.
George:	Now this is the last day in December. My Mom just got to settle in, she's talking with my aunt and uncle when there's this big noise. Explosions coming from the street, loud factory whistles. And the three boarders are running from the bedroom they share and grabbing pots and pans, coats over their long johns as they go out. My Mom is scared. This is the way, her sister tells her, New Year's Eve is celebrated in America.
Bob:	And it still is.
George:	God Bless America.
Bob:	Amen.

Uranium The New Yellow Gold

The TV on the wall is blaring commercials. There's no game just commercials talking about the coming World's Series. Two women are seated at a table chatting and having a drink. The packages next to them show that they have been shopping, Three men in work clothes are sitting at the bar having a conversation. The topic is gold. They're talking about going into the hills and panning for gold now that it's over one thousand dollars an ounce. One of the men called Bob

"Hey Bob, know anything about gold?"

Bob: Not much except I see you have a gol filling. Don't smile at muggers. Just joking.

Talk to Huey at the end of the bar. He's a prospector from year one. They call Huey to join them in a drink to pick his brains. Huey is an octogeranian weather beaten character with white hair and a long white beard. He could pass for Santa except for the long brown streak of tobacco juice stain from spit running down his beard. H ejoined the men and gladly accepted the drink offered.

"Fellows, my prospecting days are over. I'm now living on social security. I dug the yellow stuff when it was 36 bucks an ounce. Once followed a gold dredge in Montana and panned what they threw away. Made 20 dollars a day. Not bad. Then I hit a good vein by a railroad trestle. I was doing fine until the Santa Fe r.r. noticed the train trembled when it passed over the bridge. They hauled me into court. The judge looked at me and took pity. Go take your mule and dig someplace else he told me.

"Did you ever hunt uranium?"

"As a matter of fact I did back in the early 40's. I met Paddy Martinez who was the first person to discover uranium in the U S. This is the story he told me....

"I was sleeping off a drunk at a table. Now Indians were not allowed to be served alcohol in those days but my being a half-breed I could get a drink. I wasn't asleep when two well dressed men suits and ties came into the bar. Through the corner of my eye I saw them put some yellow rock on the bar and say the government is looking for this rock and would pay 10 thousand dollars to anyone who knew where to find it. I knew where there was plenty. When I was camped on Haystack Mountain working for the Santa Fe R.R. I saw that canary yellow rock.

The next morning I rode my horse there and loaded my saddlebags with the rocks. I brought it to their office, threw it on the desk and said,"Is this what you want?" Yes! They were excited. Take us there! How do you want the money? If they paid me all at once I knew I would squander it all in a month so I said break it down to so much a month. I took them to the spot and from thaty day I was known as the highest paid worker for the Santa Fe RR because it took me a few seconds to sign my check every month. Huey: I got to know Paddy quite well. He told me he was medicine man for his tribe. "When you're sick come see me. Bring a half gallon of wine and I'll sing, dance, and pray for you all night." This colorful character died at 88.

" Quite a tale Huey, but did you find any uranium?" asked Bob

No. I had 12 claims in the four corner area, y'know where the 4 western states meet. I went over it all with my geiger counter found nothing. Some geologist from the East who was living in a trailer with his wife and kids came and offered me 12 grand for my claims. I thought I had a live one so I took the money and went through it like a drunken sailor on Liberty. Later I found out he sold the claims to the government for 3 million. The claims were in the area where uranium was so the government was buying up all adjacent claims, irregardless. I went on a three day drunk.

Bob and the three men said, "We don't blame you Huey, we'd do the same. But you'd probably do the same with the 3 million that you did with the 12 grand."

Huey: "That I would fellows, no doubt about it, but it would take a few weeks longer.."

Patricio "Paddy" Martinez (1881-1969), American prospector and sheepherder, discovered uranium at Haystack Mountain, near Grants, New Mexico in 1950. This was the first discovery in the Grants Uranium District, and led to a uranium boom that lasted almost 30 years.

Martinez's discovery, on Santa Fe Railroad land, was developed into the Haystack mine. He was hired by the railroad and Anaconda Mining Company as a uranium scout for $400 per month, a good salary then.

Martinez, a Navajo of Mexican descent, and native New Mexican, became famous for his discovery. He was the subject of feature articles in *Time*, *Life*, *True West* and *Reader's Digest* magazines. Martinez was fluent in the Navajo, Laguna (Keresan), Sparfish and English languages. He was a medicine man and a leader in his community.

His tombstone at Grants Memorial Cemetery simply reads, 'Paddy Martinez 1881 - 1969 Uranium Pioneer.' He rests a stones throw from Paddy Martinez Park, where children play. He was inducted into the National Mining Hall of Fame in 1992.

Counterfeiting

The government always has to be one step ahead. With modern technology it's easy to make bogus bills, even banks get stuck with phoneys. Nat was telling Bob about his experience with a fake ten.

Nat: I bought my daily paper and racing form as usual from the corner drug store and paid with a ten spot. The clerk told me after a precursory exam that the bill was counterfeit.

Bob: What did he do?

Nat: He said he'd cash it anyway and pass it on. So I took my papers and change and went home. That ten came from the bank along with other bills when I cashed my social security check so I went to the bank and told them about it. When they asked to see it I told them I spent it. I asked them if I did bring it in would they give me a bona-fide bill to replace it and they said, "No"

Bob: Good you spent it.

Nat: Otherwise I couldn't order another drink. Put a head on this beer, Bob.

Bob: Gladly.

Nat: Reminds me, Bob, years ago we had a church member who made counterfeit nickels.

Bob: Nickels?

Nat: Nickels. He put nickels in the church collection basket, paid all his bills in nickels. He was our favorite visitor because he gave us handfuls when he came.

Bob: Was he ever caught?

Nat: Yeah, and he was sent up the river but not for long. His nickels were made even better than the mints, in fact, they released him and put him to work there.

Bob: How about that! Did they pay his salary in nickels?

Nat: Hell no!!

The Coney Island Treatment:

    Our Merchant Marine is rapidly disappearing, ships are transferring to different flags of nations like Panama and Columba to avoid paying top wages to non-union seamen. Leroy is a fortunate sailor who still makes the "married man's run" that's from New York to Bremerhaven, Germany. His run of 14 days is from the U.S. and his wife and kids in Connecticut and to a girlfrien in Germany.

    But tonight, Leroy enters the bar with a very young brunette.

Bob: Hello Leroy. Long time no sea. Get it, sea?

Leroy: Funny. Hey, I want you to meet Daisey here. Now ain't she a doll? We'll have two Buds Bob

Bob: Pleased to meet you, Daisy, but you don't look old enough to be served.

Daisy: Here's my driver's license. I'm 22.

Bob: Okay, but you do look younger.

Daisy: Thanks. I work for the Telephone Company and I'm crazy about Leroy.

Bob: (Wonders what this short plain-looking guy has going for him--wife and family, girlfriend and now this?) Well enjoy your beers.

Daisy: Oh I wish Leroy would give up sailing, get a job here we can get married. I don't see enough of him the way it is now.

Leroy: You know honey, I got 20 years seniority. Where can I make the big bucks I'm making now? If I got a job now I'd have to start on the bottom and work for peanuts.

Daisy: I can't help it Leroy. When you're gone I'm afraid some bimbo over there in Europe will get her claws in you. I don't want to lose you.

Leroy: Fat chance, baby. When we're in port, why I don't even leave the ship. I just look forward to coming back to you.

Daisy: I'm happy to hear that Leroy. If ever I find you cheating on me I'll give you the Coney Island Treatment.

Bob: What's that, Daisy?

Daisy: I'll get my brother and his Italian friends to take him to the beach on Coney Island some dark night,

./   ....roll him in the sand......

Bob: I wonder (to himself with a grin).....

..Did Leroy ever get to "enjoy" the sands of Coney Island? I remember Miley, the brakeman on the Santa Fe RR who was in the VA hospital in Albuqueque recoverying from a mild stroke. He had a wife and kids in El Paso, another family in Albuqueque, and another family in Santa fe. How he managed to spend his time between them in beyond my feeble comprehension. But he could really Imitate the sound of a train whistle. When he came down the hall in the ward we actually felt a train was coming. Miley refused all pain killers. He excercised his limbs and walked out of the hospital without a noticable limp. Amazing guy!

Tatoos Anyone?

Bob: Nice to see you Sylvia, the usual today?

Sylvia: Make it a double. I need it after what I went through this afternoon.

Bob: Tell me about it.

Sylvia: I always wanted a tatoo but I'm deathly afraid of needles. Somehow I got up enough nerve and had this tatoo done. See?

Bob: (Looking at her upper arm) That's a beautiful canary

Sylvia: It's like my Tweety at home. My pet, five years now. Some people have a dog, love-on-four-legs. I have this little bird, love-on-wings. Hey, over there! Ed, come look at my tatoo!

Ed: Ah yes! A work of art!

Bob: You know about tatoos?

Ed: Sure. Got one myself. Wanna hear about it?

Bob: Yeah, why not?

Ed: Back in '42 our Navy ship was going through Panama Canal and all my shipmates went ashore and got their tatoos. I'm like Sylvia here, scared of needles. But my buddies got me to get one.

Bob: I don't see any on you.

Ed: Oh it's a big one. A red rose on the cheek of my ass. Only now it's a long stem. Wanna see it? (Starts to pull down his pants.

Sylvia: NO No. We'll take your word it's lovely. Now pull up your britches!

The Bastard of a Teacher:

Marty: Hey Bob, a teacher in this newspaper here accused of having sex with a student. Seems to be a lot of that lately.

Bob: You were a teacher for what 30 years, Marty? Anything like that happened when you were working?

Marty: If there was, I never heard about it. One time when I was first teaching I was put on the carpet for using inappropriate language in class.

Bob: In the time I've known you, Marty, I never even heard you cuss.

Marty: My first job, teaching only three weeks, I was summoned over the loudspeaker to go to the principal's office. I saw little Sidney, his Mom and the principal all looking grim. 'Sidney says you used a bad word in class yesterday' this from the principal. And I tell him, 'No sir, in fact I even teach the children to say that when angry to say, "Cheese and Rice" instead of taking the name of the lord in vain. So what was it I supposedly said,?

Sidney: Bastard.

They all looked daggers at me.

Bob: What then, Marty?

Marty: Well, Sidney tells us that a classmate, Margaret, asked was I married. I said no, I was a bachelor.

Sidney's Mom and the principal laughed. Then they explained to the lad the meaning plus the pronunciation of "bachelor"

Bob: Well that kid probably heard the word a lot in his home.

Marty: No doubt (laughs)

Bob: On the house, Marty.

Marty: Here's to all bastards!

Out of the Closet:

Kevin: Pour me a boilermaker, Bob. I need a stiff drink.

Bob: Here you go.

Kevin: My son's getting married.

Bob: That's good news.

Kevin: Yes, but not good.

Bob: You don't like the bride-to-be?

Kevin: Not at all.

Bob: Why? You don't have to live with her, he does.

Kevin: It's not a her; it's a him. My son, Brian is marrying his friend, Byron.

Bob: Oh.

Kevin: Last weekend they both came to visit us. As usual the good conversation, some laughs, food and drinks and then they dropped the bomb. I was shocked, Maggie too. Our four kids, well they accepted it, congratulated them. I didn't know what to say. I left the room. They went back to Massachusetts where they live and work. You know religion has a hold on me, altar boy growing up, even thinking of becoming a Catholic priest--changed my mind though. Yet you know that in the Bible homosexuality is forbidden.

Bob: Well Kevin, I know my Bible, don't see nothing--but remember the Bible was written years and years ago. These are modern times. And throughout history there had been gay clergy, bishops, ministers and even popes.

And the most creative artists like DaVinci, Michaelanglo and others. And even today some who are in our government in Washington who have come out. Now Kevin, you don't love your son any less do you? Accept it. And love them. They're God's children.

Kevin: Yeah, well--

Bob: I remember you were all-star athlete in school. Your Brian marched to a different drummer, never went for sports, had his music, performing in school plays. But he graduated college, you barely finished high school. And I remember your bragging about your son right here in this pub, many times.

Kevin: That I did. And he was never a problem to us growing up. May have had my suspicions, brushed them off. My God! Oh! How he must have suffered, afraid to say anything all those years. Well, Bob, thanks. Yeah, I'll go to the ceremony, accept Byron into the family.

Bob: Good move. (Fills his drink)

Kevin: Here's to my son- and son-in-law!

Jury Duty

Bob: What are you doing here, Walter? I thought you were picked for jury duty and would be serving on some juicy murder case.

Walter: Never happen, Bob, besides I didn't want those boring fender bender cases. I was once on a trial that was interesting. It lasted two weeks. A black man slit the throat of another black. Didn't kill him but left a jagged scar from ear to ear. He pleaded "not guilty". We had trouble convincing one sweet little white lady because she couldn't believe one person could be that cruel to another human being. We were all going to go along with her and let him go just to get out and go home but a Black jury member convinced us all, including her, that the man was guilty without a doubt.

Bob: Tell me Walter, what was the sentence?

Walter: He got time in the iron motel again. It wasn't his first violent episode. The judge told us later that he was guilty. He had to plead not guilty because he beat up a girl friend with a hammer and had that charge to face. The sweet little old lady said," Goodness, I'm so glad we made the right decision"

Bob: So back to now. How did you get out of jury duty today?

Walter: When the lawyers questioned me about what makes me happy I replied Staying away from doctors, lawyers, and used car dealers like the gentleman on my right. The judge smiled and said, "I wish I could say that." After the laughter subsided the lawyers agreed I should leave.

Bob: Stay happy Walter. Glad I wasn't included with those three.

Walter: Never happen Bob, believe me.

Art For Art's Sake?

Bob: How's it going fellas? (greets Ian and Marty) How's the art class, drawing anything besides flies?

Ian: Fun-ny. No more still life. This week we're into the nude female figure.

Bob: Sounds interesting.

Marty: We got a real live model, Bob. Beautiful girl, built! Poses, not a stitch of clothes on. Our class is 14 guys and 2 girls. The teacher is male. What we do is we concentrate on our drawing. After the model is finished posing she comes to chat with us. This is while she's getting in her clothes. Well, the minute she starts pulling up her nylon stockings, then her Panties, we get instant hard-ons.

Bob: (Laughs) Well it's not only clothes that make the man, women too!

Ian: Next week we're drawing a nude male model.

Bob: And the two women in the class?

Ian: If they get turned on, Bob, there's just no way we can see a " wide on".

Bob: Too bad you can't. It's one advantage the opposite sex has over you guys. Your excitement shows.

Ian: I wish she was less friendly. Another beer, Bob!

A Puerto Rican Poem

Tom: Hiya Bob! Gimmie a beer! I just got back from Puerto Rico. Didn't do so hot at the dice table in the casino so I had to hole up in a flea bag hotel. Not the Hilton by any means but surprisingly it had business cards on the desk in the front entrance. I picked one up and glanced at the back of the card. There was a poem that zeroed in on my philosophy of life. Wanna hear it?

Bob: Sure, Tom, go ahead. I'm listening.

Tom: Here goes: uncouth, I mean unquote:

When I'm in a drunken mood, I gamble, chase, and drink

When I'm in a pensive mood, I grumble, sit, and think.

When my moods are over, and from this world I pass.

Bury me with my face turned down,

So the world can kiss my ass.

Bob: I like that, Tom, but I remember you once telling me you wanted to be cremated and your ashes scattered from a plane at 30 thousand feet, you being a former airforce pilot.

Tom: Did I ? Yeah, I forgot. Anyway it still jibes with my philosophy of coming and going. We're hatched, matched, and dispatched.

Bob: True, Tom, We aspire, prespire, expire.

San Gennaro's Feast

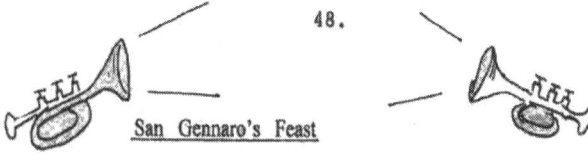

Living in America one can enjoy many different ethnic events, like Polish weddings, Jewish Bar Mitzvahs, German octoberfests, Mexican Cinco de Mayos, just to name a few. One Italian celebration, the San Gennaro feast is one you shouldn't miss. It's an 11 day event Sept. 16-26 of eating, drinking, dancing in the roped off streets of NY City's little Italian section.

Bob: Did you go to the feast last week, Don? I know you're not Italian but you love Italian food.

Don: You bet I did, Bob. Besides the pasta I also love the dark-haired Italian girls Especially those who don't shave their legs or armpits. That really turns me on.

Bob: I thought you were afraid of the dark and only chased blondes. Ha!

Don: Blondes, brunettes, redheads, I like them all. But that night I did meet a gorgeous blonde. She stood out in the crowd like a dirty fingernail in third grade. She had a body that wouldn't quit.

Bob: Tell me about her.

Don: She had a bandage on her nose which gave me the opening gambit. My sister had a nose job and was bandaged like that so I walked up to her and asked, "How was the operation"? She smiled and filled me in on the details. Her Dad was with the FBI in Miami, Fla. And paid for her to go to NYC and have it done by an expensive specialist. He arranged for his 25 year old daughter to stay at a Nun's retreat in Newark NJ where she would be safe. She showed me a foto of her nose before the operation. Only a small bump, hardly noticeable. Vanity! I thought, Vanity and vexation of spirit (Eccles came to mind). Well we had a great time pigging out on the food, drinks, dancing the Tarantella to the music of street musicians. Later I drove her to the Nun's place. We started to have a romantic session in the car but were interrupted by a rainstorm that turned into hail. I worried about the roof of the car because it was my brother's Studebaker. I was using it since he was in Nam. We said Goodnight and she promised to call me.

Bob: Did she call?

Don: She did. a few days later. She needed a ride to Manhattan. It seemed she was drinking beer with her girlfriends and got sick. She went to throw up and the seat of the commode fell and hit her on the nose.

Bob: Don't tell me!

Don: Yep. It raised a bump in the same place. I drove her and waited outside in my car. She emerged rather disconsolate. Looks like she would have to continue staying in Newark for another week or so.

Bob: How did it turn out?

Don: I dunno. Never saw her again. Got me thinking...Where would Durante have been had he fixed his snozzola?

Bob: Good question, Don!

Bad News Travels Fast

On a Saturday afternoon we find Bartender Bob setting up for the big night crowd. He was signing an order for two just delivered kegs of beer when a well dressed man walked in. "Something strong," he ordered. This wasn't a boilermaker type more like college. Bob drew up a Scotch and Soda for him. The delivery man left. The man leaned over the bar. He wanted to talk. He gave his name "Brian" and with the surname Bob recognized at once, this guy writes the commentaries on the editorial page of the area newspaper. Hey, bartenders read newspapers too! Brian began by saying that the Friday afternoon crew of reporters and editors had gone home for the weekend and he and the managing editor Howard ere the only ones left. He looked up to see a man at his desk, a desperate look on his face.

"I want to keep something out of the paper," the man said,"My daughter is getting married tomorrow" Continuing barely able to talk "Everyone, wife and all are at the reception hall getting things ready. I was home alone when two men came up the walk. They were in uniform. Being a WW2 vet, I knew what it was about----our only son Peter. I accepted the large envelope and the flag folded in a triangle. My daughter must'nt know. She should have her wedding day. I know thw military notifies the newspapers of the men killed in action. If only it could be left out......She loved her twin brother so much!" He sobbed. "Our only son. Peter."

Bob drew another Scotch and Soda for Brian.

Brian: I checked the AP with Howard and nothing came in as yet so I assured the father
       that we would mark the news for the Tuesday edition so his daughter would have

her day. I cried with the father before he left.

Bob: That was the humane thing to do, Brian.

Brian: Damn the war! It takes lives of young men for what? To satisfy the greed of old men. I'll write my next article about the futility and stupidity of wars especially the two we're helplessly mired in now.

Bob: Good idea, Brian, I'm looking forward to reading it.

From 9 To 90

Alan returned to NJ after spending six years out West. There he got involved in a mining company with three others, but decided to leave after one of the partners sold a piece of land they didn't own to a State Senator. All they owned were the mineral rights, nothing else. Alan lost ten grand but decided not to stick around and went back East to lick his wounds. His aging parents were glad to see him and so were many of his boyhood chums. The ones he visited were all married, routinized by punching time clocks in dead-end factory jobs and drinking beer, watching sports on TV at home every night. Alan at 29 wasn't quite ready for that. He believed in "Happiness of pursuit" and often quotes his favorite poem

>   The time I spent in wooing, In watching and pusuing
>   The light that lies in women's eyes
>   Has been my hearts undoing
>   Tho' wisdom oft has sought me, I scorned the lore it brought me
>   My only books were women's looks
>   And folly's all they taught me.

Dust and feathers settle down but not yet Alan. His religion's Wine, women, song. The wine and song are available but so far no woman in the three weeks he's been back. Driving past the old defunk Esso station on busy Rt,1 Alan decides to drop in on Ol' Mr.Schultz who lives there alone. The place is like a Norman Rockwell painting. Rusted gas pump, run down station, crumbling tourist cabins in back, old man in overalls feeding chickens.. He greets Alan and offers him schnapps which Alan graciously accepts. Schulz's Kids want him to sell the place and move in with them but he's German and stubborn, He and Alan talk about the nostalgic old times when gas was 12 cents

Gallon and Alan always gassed up there. Schulz closed his station years ago and lives alone with his animals. Alan quickly brought him up-to-date on his activities.

What happened to the motorcycle shop next to your place? Asked Alan.

Schultz: Gone. Too many under-age girls hanging around. The cops closed the place. moved to PA someplace. Hey, Alan, you got girl?

Alan: No.

Schlutz: I know nice one. Give you blow-job. Three dolla. I call. She come.

Alan: Sounds good. Call her.

Schultz uses the wall phone. Dials a number. Tells Alan she come Visions of the young intern and Clinton dance in Alan's brain. The Anticipation is almost too much. Here comes the bus! It stops in front. The lone passenger alighting is an old bent over gray lady more at the age of collapse than consent. She hobbles toward the station.

Yikes! It suddenly dawns on Alan. Dumb me! She's in HIS age group! I should have realized that. She's warmly greeted by Schultz and introduced to Alan who smiles and exchanges pleasantries.

Bob: What happened next, Alan?

Alan: What could I do? Didn't want to hurt Grandma's feelings. I like women from 9 to 90. This one's closer to 90 but at least she's not San Quenton Quail so the two of us went into one of the cabins. Inside was a single bed, toilet, And a few pieces of furniture. On the dresser was radio that you put a quarter in for 15 minutes of music. No TV. Getting down to business she asked me how I wanted it. I couldn't see Granny giving me a hummer so I said the usual way.

She started to strip down to her black bra and black panties, Her skin was white in contrast. A surprisingly fine figure. No stretch marks.cellulose. I Undressed ready to press the flesh. She took a condom from her purse and told me always to use one because of all the diseases today. Good advice.

Schultz: Was she good, Alan? Like young girl? Better! I said. She was great! It's not The greatest beauties that inspire the most profound passions I found out. She showed me some new wrinkles! I gave her a ten spot. Schultz asked me what I meant by wrinkles but he's like the English.

Bob: I know what you mean. Those two never get it the first time. Good story Alan!

An "a-cute" Observation??

During the Depression of the 30's you were lucky to have a job. Teachers were paid in I.O.U.s because cities were broke. You had to pay to get a policeman's job. When Larry got his teaching degree in 1970 his Mom, depression day mentality, Said she would give the commissioner $100 to get a teaching job for him. Larry laughed and told his Mom that times have changed.....or did they? Today it looks like history is repeating. With the sour economy teachers are being axed. More pressure to produce is put on those working as Larry is finding out with the constant observations and evaluations. Larry repairs to the local bar after a grueling day teaching fifth graders.

Bob: The usual, Larry?

Larry: Yeah, Bob, easy on the suds this time.

Bob: How's teaching the little midgets today?

Larry: Getting rougher, Bob. Too many chiefs, not enough Indians. Ten teachers were let go this year due to the economy. They should get rid of administrators not teachers. Too many demands and pressure on us. Sometimes I wish I stayed in the Navy. Today the principal AND the superintendent both came into my classroom for an observation. I've been here 20 years and this is the first time the superintendent came into our school!

Bob: How did it go ?

Larry: I foxed them both, Bob. Before they came in I told the kids that we would review what we learned in American history. I said I'd ask questions. Those who knew the right answer, raise your right hand. Those who didn't, raise your left hand.

Bob: Sounds interesting...What happened next?

Larry: The two were amazed. Never had they seen such unbridled enthusiasm in a classroom with all students responding waving their hands to be called upon and all answering correctly!

They left looking mesmerized.

Bob: Think they'll wise up?

Larry: Hell no. If they had any brains they'd be in a classroom teaching, Bob.

A Mass Murderer:

Bob: Look at those two guys at that table. Play chess here every night this week. Buy a beer and nurse it for hours Do you play chess, George?

George: Tell you what, I had the fever one time. Played every chance I got. It was an obsession just like those two birds there. You know, chess and music are universal. I traveled through many countries not able to speak the tongues but because I played chess and, too, my having my guitar with me, I got to enjoy a lot of hospitality. I was invited into many homes for dinner and had no problem socializing.

Bob: Do you still play chess?

George: Chess, never again. My guitar I strum when I feel blue.

Bob: Why not the chess?

George: A few years back this guy, Sam and I would play a lot of chess. Even at parties, we'd be in a corner at our game, everyone else drinking and dancing. This Sam, he had a genius I.Q. College graduate, several degrees. But his wife was the breadwinner, two bright beautiful girls in grade school. He tried teaching but quit then real estate but gave that up.

Bob: You're a regular guy, maybe no genius, no offense, but did you ever get to beat him?

George: Believe it or not, yes Bob. I read books on chess the maneuvers. I felt we were evenly matched. Then one night

Bob: about 2 a.m. it all--
Why, what happened?

George: My wife and I were asleep when we heard a knock on the door. She told me to go see who it is. I put my bathrobe on. It's the police. They tell me they're looking for Sam. I asked them what for? They tell me that they found his father and mother and sister murdered. Did they think Sam killed them? They couldn't say. They wanted to know if I knew where to find him. I told them try the chess & checker place on 42nd st. in Manhattan.

Bob: Did he do it? I mean, his family like that?

George: The next day headlines in the papers, manhunts in New York and other states. The news reports that Sam got in a rage because the father wouldn't give him money and he had bludgened the family. There were two Sam headlines, at the same time the 'Son of Sam' killings were going on in Brooklyn.

Bob: Wow. Did they nab this guy?

George: Well not at once. Three weeks go by, my wife and I are in fear all the while, what if he shows up at our home? Finally they get him. It's at the chess and checker place I told them about. They were watching it all along and then he shows up.

Bob: What happened with him?

George: He got one to 20 years on three counts. A few years ago we learned he died in prison. We don't know about his wife and daughters. We lost contact with them.

Bob: Now I get the drift why you don't play chess.

George: If I'm gonna play anything, it's pinochle.

Bob: Why?

Because that's what my Pop was playing when he died. He was with his retired cronies, suddenly stood up then sat down and that was it. At the wake I asked one oldtimer from the cardplaying group, what kind of a hand did my Pop have? He said, oh a good hand, went out like a sport.

Bob: Well now, that's for me too. I sure would like to faze out the same way, George. But nobody got a contract with God, do they?

George: That's right. Lemme have another beer.

Homer

Bob: Thanks Homer for that painting of a horse rearing up. You see it there on the wall. Lot of cowboys who come in here say it's so realistic. Have a drink on the house.

Homer: Thanks Bob.

Bob: I didn't know you painted as well as writing poetry. Where do you get your colors?

Homer: I mix them from the earth mostly. Some I have to buy

Bob: You are very talented. You never said, but have you been married?

Homer: Once. She left me, said I was spending more time on my book than with her. Took my writings, a trunk full and burned it all and left.

Bob: What was your book about?

Homer: A family, "The Last of the Ilusons" who left Scotland and settled in the West. I didn't try to write it again.

Bob: What about other writing?

Homer: I once wrote a book I called, "A Boy Who Was Traded for a Mule", true story. The boy raised by the Apaches, a tribe the government was determined to eliminate. The president himself, at that time, authorized the offers for Apache scalps, $50 for squaws, $100 for men and $25 for children. Well, I took my book to a pocketbook company, told me it was well-written but had no sex in it and sex sells. Said it would make a good kid's book. But I didn't pursue that.

Bob: Where's the book now?

Homer: I don't know. Somewhere back in New Mexico.

Bob: I got one of the many poems you gave me that I keep right here on hand and read when it's slow in here. It's great stuff, not like the June, moon, spoon junk they call poetry today especially in songs.

EPHEMERA

An ephemeral gnat defied life's sea
As he rode on the crest of a wave,
I shall know no God or fear said he
Ye fools who do - I shall enslave.
I shall know no soul nor reverence
But with fervid frenzy I'll condense
Earth's riches into dollars and cents;
I'll store them all behind my fence.

2.

With cunning of my mighty brain
I shall the roaring rivers chain,
The savage beasts now flee in pain
From the jungles I have drained.
With trickery of my mighty stealth
I shall even deal with death...
With treachery, war, or automat
Fast on my road to wealth.

3..

I'll write your laws, rule the land
Even hold your future in my hand.
Machine and science I shall command
I'm a billionaire; a superman.
Great pyramids I now shall build
In cities to be named for me...
Or factories with my workers filled -
Fools I cheat so cunningly.

4.

I'm conqueror too of the seven seas
I've charted the moon and the Pleiades
I've beaten the tropics and Arctic's freeze
I'll take from Life just what I please.
Yet secretly I've left one fear
I'll somehow pull it's sting
Whenever death draws near...
For I am a money king.

5.

The cosmic clock had barely ticked
A score of years flashed by...
The great one's mighty brain seemed tricked
None knew the reason why.
Could not some lesser mortal lend
His blood to give less pain?
Must one so great as he had been
Lose all the wealth he'd gain?
Could not his gold, his miser's gold
Buy serums that would lenghten life?.
Take back the treasures that he stole
Relieve him of those fears and strife?

6.

The aged God smote his withered cheek
Asked in a voice cruel and cold...
Aren't you the one who cursed the weak
Who others- bought and sold?
Come little fool who tore my breast
You who stole my power free...
Within my arms there's room and rest
For ye little men like thee.

7.

I'll condemn you to a darkened pit
For you go no man knows where...
Fate shall find someone to sit
There in your princely chair.
...Far down below another groaned
Took out his book and moaned:
He who is coming worries me well
I fear he'll cheat me out of my Hell.

8.

I'll bank my fires to burn him slow
Again he shall be dust...
Then I shall let the bellows blow
Away this fool unjust.
Poor, silly, weak, morbid thing!
Better you had kept your tail and tree...
Than vain attempts the Gods to bring
Into your short life of agony.

9.

Better the maker had kept the mold

Than this tiny speck of dust I hold...

For death knows no class or royal state

It shows no favor, it knows no hate.

Yet shares with rich or poor its fate

A quiet sleep where storms abate...

For who has seen a pearly gate

To six feet of sod------earth's estate.

                              Loco Lobo

Homer: Here's another one for you, Bob, I copied this from a very old church in Bath, North Carolina.

G O PLACIDLY AMID THE NOISE & HASTE, & REMEMBER WHAT PEACE THERE MAY BE IN SILENCE. AS FAR AS POSSIBLE WITHOUT surrender be on good terms with all persons. Speak your truth quietly & clearly; and listen to others, even the dull & ignorant; they too have their story. ❧ Avoid loud & aggressive persons, they are vexations to the spirit. If you compare yourself with others, you may become vain & bitter; for always there will be greater & lesser persons than yourself. Enjoy your achievements as well as your plans. ❧ Keep interested in your own career, however humble; it is a real possession in the changing fortunes of time. Exercise caution in your business affairs; for the world is full of trickery. But let this not blind you to what virtue there is; many persons strive for high ideals; and everywhere life is full of heroism. ❧ Be yourself. Especially, do not feign affection. Neither be cynical about love; for in the face of all aridity & disenchantment it is perennial as the grass. ❧ Take kindly the counsel of the years, gracefully surrendering the things of youth. Nurture strength of spirit to shield you in sudden misfortune. But do not distress yourself with imaginings. Many fears are born of fatigue & loneliness. Beyond a wholesome discipline, be gentle with yourself. ❧ You are a child of the universe, no less than the trees & the stars; you have a right to be here. And whether or not it is clear to you, no doubt the universe is unfolding as it should. ❧ Therefore be at peace with God, whatever you conceive Him to be, and whatever your labors & aspirations, in the noisy confusion of life keep peace with your soul. ❧ With all its sham, drudgery & broken dreams, it is still a beautiful world Be careful Strive to be happy

THE COOKIE JAR

Bob: Buon Giorno, Vinnie! Here's your vino rojo!

Vinnie; Thanks Bob.Salud! Your speaking Italian makes me nostalgic for the old days. I miss my folks. They didn't have much formal education but they had a lot of wisdom.
-Did I ever tell you about the cookie jar?

Bob; No, Vinnie, I'd like to hear it. Tell me.

Vinnie: We had a cookie jar on the kitchen shelf. In it was change. Everything in those days was cash on the barrelhead– no plastic credit cards. Any change was put in that jar. One day I needed money."Pop, I need money." "Go ahead son, help yourself." So I did.

A week later I went to Pop. "I need some money. Pop."

"Go ahead son, help yourself."

Two weeks later more financial need and another plea to Pop.

"Go ahead Son, help yourself.

I went to the jar again."Pop, there's no money in it."

Pop replied, "What do you expect? You always take out and never put in."

Bob: Sounds like the government.

Vinnie: Exactly! The mess we're in now.Remember that movie about Pancho Villa? The people said they needed more pesos. You want pesos? We got the printing presses- we'll print all you want.

Bob: Another government solution.

REDUCE TO THE LOWEST COMMON DENOMINATOR

Marge: Hiya Bob!

Bob: Here's your usual pick-me-up gin and tonic

Marge: Thanks Bob, good memory.

Bob: No problem, Marge, how's it going with those little midgets in grade three?

Marge: No problem with them, Bob, but the administration is putting so much pressure on us that I'd quit except we need the money. My fisherman husband doesn't work steady all year with him it's feast or famine. I need the job.

Bob: What's your beef with the bosses?

Marge: The principal we have got his job through politics, he never taught in a classroom. He's an ex-military colonel and runs a tight ship, so to speak. He even sends communiques instead of memos. Every teacher is terrified of him, me included.

Bob: The men teachers?

Marge:: Them too. Today over the speaker I was summoned to report to the office. To be reprimmanded for something no doubt. I went and stood outside the door Afraid to go in. Jack, a fellow teacher noticed me trembling outside. When I confided my fears he came up with a novel suggestion.

Bob: Tell me, I'm listening.

Marge: He told me to go in and reduce that martinet to the lowest common denominator. He said the Emperor had no clothes and like in the novel Forever Amber the king himself used a common pot so Marge, go in and picture that fat pompous Baldheaded bum naked sitting on the commode..

Bob: And did you?

Marge: Yes, Bob, and the ludicrous image set me off. I began laughing and couldn't stop' After five minutes he told me to get out.

Bob: That was good advice. It's a very good way not to be intimidated by ones in power over you. Reduce him to the lowest common denominator? I like that Marge. Once a teacher always a teacher, that's you. Hey, that can be used in any other work place as well. illegitimi non carborundum Don't let the bastards grind you down.

The World's Oldest Profession ?

Adam, Mike, Paul, and Stan, four assembly-line workers at the GM plant always repair to the watering hole across the street from the factory on pay day to have a drink. They take turns paying for the rounds and always engage in a lively bar-room debate. The world's oldest profession is the topic today.

Mike breaks out in song:

"See him seated in the House Of Commons,

Passing laws for all mankind,

While she walks the streets of London.

Selling chunks of 'er behind"

Paul: Where'd you hear that, Mike?

Mike: The British sailors. It's part of a raunchy song they sing.

Adam: I like that " selling chunks of 'er behind"

Stan– I disagree with you guys about prostitution being the oldest profession'

Begging is. A guy has to beg for it.

The men laugh.

Paul–Go into double harness, Stan, and you won't have to beg.

Stan: I'd rather beg. But speaking of begging reminds me of a time when I was living in a $2.50 a week room in Newark, NJ, going to school under the GI Bill living on $75 a month. Wanna hear about it?

Mike: Go ahead, you'll tell us anyway. Bob! Another round on me! And, Bob. stick around to hear Stan's story.

stick around to hear Stan's story.

Bob, replenishing the drinks, Go ahead, Stan, Tell us.

Stan: Like I said, I was living in the closet size furnished room. Across the hall from me, same size room, was a guy who had a girlfriend visit him almost every night. She didn't stay long, just a few minutes. No hanky panky.

Paul; What's that got to do with begging?

Stan: I'm getting to it. After she left, a dirty beat up guy in rags came out of the room and left. I was puzzled. The room was too small for two people. Every night the Same thing happened. One afternoon I saw him and asked about this. He told me that he worked at the printing shop. His girlfriend was of Italian descent, like him, and they planned to get married but he didn't make enough money at the shop. Every night, after work,. He would dress in rags and go to Penn RR Station and beg. He said he made more in one night begging than a week at the shop. Of course he never told his girlfriend.

Paul: There but for the grace of God go I. A beggar always gets my spare change.

Adam: Mine too..Sometimes I flip him a buck or two.

Bob: That's some story, Stan. Did they ever get married?

Stan: I dunno, Bob. I dropped out of school and went to Alaska. Now when I was in Alaska............

Adam, Mike, Paul in unison: Shut up Stan! Drink your beer!!!

    The four finished their drinks and left. destined to routinely return the next pay day and the next. It was a comfortable rut. But all too soon to be interrupted by the men singing songs like "Wedding Bells are breaking up that old gang of mine"

INTERMISSION

A QUICK PAUSE FOR REFILLS

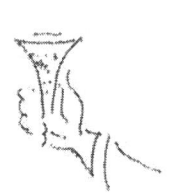

I hope you're enjoying the stories so far. Before you continue, my next episode will be coming out soon and I need stories from readers like you.

Write to me at tellittobartenderbob@gmail.com And if your story is used you'll get some $$, thanks, and a drink on the house

SLANTE! NA ZDROWIE! SKOAL! SALUD! PROSIT! KAMPAI!! TO YOUR HEALTH!!!!!

A NON-PAYING PASSENGER

Kenny: Bob, give me a Guiness stout.

Bob: Here you go, Kenny, that's you're weakness, I know.

Haven't been around lately, where've you been?

Kenny: Working in Brooklyn, Bob, taking the subway to work everyday.

Yesterday I witnessed an interesting thing on my ride to work-care to hear about it?

Bob: Yes, tell it to me.

Kenny: Well, there I was sitting, minding my own business, looking vacantly ahead like others in the subway car when my eyes focused on something moving on the fur coat of the white dowager seated across from me. She was obviously wealthy, judging by her coiffure, jewelry, And rainment but oblivious of the non-paying passenger crawling on her coat.

Bob: What was it?

Kenny: A cockroach. It wasn't moving fast, taking its sweet, old time. Seated next to her was a black woman, poorly clad, obviously headed for a poor paying menial job or the Welfare office.

I watched the roach make its way across to the shabby coat of the black woman. The haughty white woman happened to glance down and see the bug now on the black woman's coat. You should've seen the cold look on the white woman's face! It was enough to freeze strawberries!

Bob: The eyes have one language everywhere, Kenny, no need for words.

Kenny: Yeah, Bob. I felt like telling her that the roach came from her fur coat but I kept quiet, falling into the New York pattern of minding your own business.

Bob: Didn't take you long, Kenny, only one day. She was probably prejudiced anyhow and wouldn't believe you. Having two eyes but only seeing with one, being blind-sided with bigotry.

Kenny: You're right, Bob, let her enjoy her miserable prejudices. That black woman probably was superior to her in many ways. Comes the day she'll be weighed in the balance and definitely found wanting, especially in this incident.

Bob: Hey, that's philisophical Kenny, unlike you. Must be the Guiness talking.

Kenny: Wait until I drink a few more- then you should hear me!

Bob: Sorry, Kenny, my hearing aid battery just went dead.

Thety both laugh.

74.

Komashnah

  A celebration of life fo;;owing a burial of a member of the Slavonic race. Ethnic foods and liquor comprise a big feast just like an Irish Wake. People eat, drink, talk about the merits of the deceased and then go home....until the next one.

Bob: Why the black tie, Rudy?

Rudy: I just came from a Komashnah. You know what that is, don't you?

Bob: Yeah, I've served many a Slavic patron. Who died this time?

Rudy One armed John.

Bob: I heard of him. He owned a workingman's bar in Brooklyn. Very successful. Sometimes three deep at the bar. Do you know how he lost his arm? I never Knew the facts.

Rudy: I'll tell you. It happened years ago outside of Butch's poolroom. Charlie parked his five dollar Buick in front and went inside to play snooker. When he came out the junk wouldn't start. We all came out to push. I pushed on the back bumper Which was made of solid steel not plastic like today. John was pushing on the window. When the car lurched into second gear John's arm went through the glass severing an artery. I saw the blood spurt out in a stream. We tied a tourniquet and

Gangrene set in and the docs went that night to John's home to get his parents' permission to amputate. I never forgot that night. We were all outside the house. The doctors in white coats and an interpreter approached the immigrant parents who spoke no English. They were stoical and showed little emotion but you could see and almost feel the pain they were going through. John's arm was amputated above the elbow leaving a stump.

WW2 broke out soon after and we all went into the services except John. He went into various businesses, scrap metal, fish, auto tires, and bar owner. He married raised four daughters and two sons all college graduates and left a sizable inheritance To them all.

Bob: I wonder what would his life had been like had he not lost his arm?
Rudy: He'd probably be like me; discharged from the service, collecting unemployment drifting from one dead end job to another, lacking a steady female companion, and drowning in self pity.

A Lockup Lookup

Bob: Kevin! What a surprise! Back from Seattle?

Kevin: Yeah Bob, back to my boyhood town. I don't miss the town as much as I do my boyhood.

Bob: Those were the days my friend.

Kevin: From the song with the same name. Gimmie a beer.

Bob: Coming right up. Just back for a visit?

..... Not this time. Lost my job in Boeing; they fired me because of age. I'm suing them now and got a good case according to my lawyer.

Bob: Hope you win Kevin- age discrimination is in the papers a lot today. How's your folks?

Kevin: Another reason. They both need help. My Mom says old age is no fun. She's right. Dad had a bad heart attack recently.

Bob: Run into any of your old buddies?

Kevin: As a matter of fact I saw one last week. Shoey, real name Joe. We all had nicknames. I had to go to Newark and took a short cut on a service road that went past that big domed shaped state prison. They have a big farm outside the grounds where they grow vegetables. Saves money. As I drove by I spotted a familiar face among the inmates working the field. Shoey, my boyhood pal!!!
"SHOEY" I yelled He looked up and yelled back."KEVIN! COME VISIT ME! I'LL SEND YOU A PASS!" Before I could ask him what he was in for the guard waved his rifle at me to move. I left in a cloud of dust.

Bob: Did you get to visit him?

Kevin: I got the pass but before I could visit him he was already released. I ran into him on Main Street in town. Quite a story he told me. Wanna hear it?

Bob: Sure do. Tell it to me.

Kevin: Remember now this is his version...I quote:

(Shoey) I ran into Phil, you remember him. He's now the mayor of our town. You know Phil was always full of more shit than a Thanksgiving turkey- that's why he was elected. A born politician. Phil said hey buddy I'm taking my girlfriend to Angelos for pizza, why don't you get a date and join us? So I got Agnes, a bimbo I used to be intimate with and joined them. We were having a good time eating, drinking beer, and reliving old times when I got a bit horny and took Agnes to the nearby claypits. There was no moon out and it was very dark so we parked and got in the back seat to-ha!- "Put footprints on the roof". For what ever reason she said she wasn't in the mood so we got back in the front seat. In getting out of the back she fell and hit her head on the running board. Small bruise. No big deal. We went back, rejoined Phil and Mary, had a few more beers, called it a night and left. I dropped Agnes off and went home to sleep.

The next morning two cops knocked on my door. They took me in my pajamas to jail and booked me for rape. Not wanting to drag Phil in and maybe have him lose his job, I asked my lawyer for advice. He told me if I pleaded guilty it would be only six months and since I had three months in the county workhouse to my credit, I'd only have to serve three months. That sounded OK so I went with the guilty plea. The judge banged the gavel and said four years. I served every day of that four years.

Bob: Some lawyer! What bar was he admitted to? Not mine!

Did Phil ever visit Shoey in the four years?

Kevin: Not once, Bob. Knowing what a Don Juan Shoey was with the ladies I asked him About his sex life in prison. He told me he had sex with other inmates but now that he was out he was back to "females of the opposite sex" and .in fact. He had one in his furnished room he would gladly share with me. I politely refused telling him I had a steady girl which was a lie. He's somewheres now in Florida teaching scuba diving.

Bob: Scuba diving? I thought he'd be raising vegetables what with his four years " apprenticeship".

Kevin: If he messes with any of those Miami mermaids Daddy Neptune will stick the legal trident up his hamus Alabamus for another four year stretch.

Bob: It sure was a novel way to run into a friend Kevin.Hope you run into your other friends in better places than iron motels.

Kevin:I'll drink to that, Bob, put a head on this beer.

Off Her Rocker

Angelo: Shot and beer, Bob.

Bob: Righto,! How's Michael-Angelo the painter doing?

Angelo: It's Angelo, Bob. I just finished a job at a nursing home, not exactly the Sistine Chapel. What a depressing place! I hope I never wind up in one!

Bob: Me neither. My Mom was in one before she died. She was always saying,"Why doesn't God take me away from this horrible place?" He finally did after six long suffering months.

Angelo: They charge a lot of pesos to stay in there too. They grab your home and whatever assets you have. And for what? Most of the people there are senile and mentally lacking anyway, like the old lady in the rocking chair yesterday.

Bob: What about her?

Angelo: She was a frail, sweet looking old gal slowly rocking and watching us paint. She seemed to be troubled about something so I went to her and she told me. Care to hear what was on her mind, or what was left of it?

Bob: Tell it to me, Angelo

Angelo: She said,"Mister, can you do something about those mice? All night they keep coming out of that hole in the wall and making noises. It keeps me awake and I can't sleep all night."

"Where?" I asked.

She pointed to the wall."There!"

I saw only a blank wall. To humor her I took my paint brush, dipped it in the pail, and smeared the wall inb the spot she indicated. I generously gave it two coats.

Bob: Then what?

Angelo: We came back the next day to finish the job. There she was sitting and rocking. A cherubic smile on her wrinkled face.

"Mister, thank you for covering that hole. All night I heard them trying to get in but you covered it so they couldn't. Thanks to you I had a good night's sleep. Thank you, thank you!!!"

Bob: You missed your calling, Angelo. Hang up your brush and hang up a shingle.

"ANGELO PSYCHOLOGIST"

Angelo: I'll stick to painting, Bob. To be a psychologist and earn your rubber hammer, You know, to test knee reflexes, takes a lot of time, money, and study. Most of the ones who choose that path have mental problems they think they can solve by going into that field.

Bob: True, Angelo, and what about you? No problems?

Angelo: Hell yes. Like you and others. That's Life. Wanna hear about mine?

Bob: Later, Angelo, I gotta see what's with that guy at the end of the bar. He's been crying in his beer for the past hour.

Angelo: It's you, not me who should hang out a shingle. Thanks for listening!

<u>Proverbs</u>   Do something or get off the pot

A closed mouth gathers no flies   At night all cats look gray

the higher the ape climbs the more   The masses are asses
he shows his bare ass

                                                                                             No news is good news

ask about your neighbors before you buy the house

God helps the poor man.He protects him from expensive sins

It's a slow afternoon at the bar. Only one customer nursing a beer, reading a book, paying no attention to the TV that's blaring overhead. Bob goes over to hom and asks,"Chad, you always have your nose buried in a book; what are you reading this time?"

Chad: "A book of proverbs,Bob."

Bob: "There's a lot of wisdom in them, Chad, my folks always had one for every occasion. I still remember a few of my Mom's."On the thief's head the hat is burning" and "Once bitten by a snake you're even afraid of a bullfrog." Somehow she fit them into the problem at hand.It always made me think about the situation and act wisely...sometimes.

Chad: Here's one for you, Bob. A lad tells his father he's going out into the world to seek his fortune. Father admonishes him with "A rolling stone gathers no moss".It doesn't deter the lad and he takes off. Years later he returns in a stretch limo bedecked in fine clothing wearing gold jewelry obvioulsly very rich.The father says, "Like I always said , son, It's the wandering bee that gets the honey."

Bob: Any proverb in there Chad about having another beer?

Chad: Off hand I don't know, Bob. Pour me another glass and I'll

do some searching. Somewhere in this book I saw "Drink to elevation".

That sounds like a good proverb. I'll look for the rest of it.

Bob: Happy hunting Chad- or should I call you the "Solomon of Saloons?"

Chad: Don't exalt me, Bob, just call me Chad, I'm a humble guy y'know.

83.

La Serenata (The serenade)

In Mexico the serenade is a romantic custom to win the heart of a senorita. A guy hires mariachis to play romantic songs in the early hours outside the bedroom window of his sweetheart. (A practice we could also use in our country, No?)

Bob: Here's your Corona Especial, Willie.

Willie: Gracias, Roberto, tu eres un caballero muy simpatico.

Bob: Thanks for the compliment, I think. You spent some time in Mexico I gather?

Willie: Yeah, Bob. I love their food, music, and senoritas, especially the Senoritas, in fact, I was sweet on one. Care to hear about it?

Bob: Sure, Willie, tell it to me.

Willie: I was in a music store in Chihuahua looking to buy a record of the latest hit. I asked the clerk for "Mamacita corazon" Maria, a young beautiful senorita overheard me and laughed ."Senor, you mean Amor, not Mama cita. The clerk joined in the laughter. Laughter, Bob, Is the shortest distance between strangers

Bob: And Freud believed laughter is closely intertwined with lust.

Willie: I don't doubt that, Bob. Maria and I hit it off immediately. She invited me to dinner at her home and I met her entire family which was large, believe me. Her Dad was mayor of the city, a rich and very powerful politician.

When I returned to Albuqueque where I was a student at the university, I corresponded with her. During school breaks I'd go visit but I could never get her alone- chaperones were always present, a Mexican custom I hated. Then one day it hit the fan.

Bob: What did?

Willie: Our budding romance, that's what. It was nipped in the bud. My buddy Raul and I went to Mexico on our break. We were talking to two senoritas on the street when Maria and her sister happened to drive by. She saw us laughing and having fun. Mexican women can be very jealous, you know.

when I came to her house that night she refused to see me. Later that same night Raul and I crashed a wedding. There I met a tool and die maker from California who was a guest. I told him about my plight and he suggested a Serenata. Hey, Ill try anything once! So at two AM we hailed two taxis to transport us and the three street musicians we hired, to her house. First we had To stop at the police station to pay "multa" permission which was only seventy five cents.

We all piled out of the taxis in front of her bedroom window. With a case of beer we were all set.

What shall we play, senor? Despierta? (wake up) Tu solo tu?(You only you) Dulce amor de mi vida? (sweet love of my life)

I told them to play "Carabina treinta treinta" (carbine 30/30) a ballad she knew I liked and she'd know it'd be me.

It was long like some Country Western songs. After they played it, no lights appeared. No maiden on the balcony.Nothing. Nada.

"What song now,senor?"

Maybe she didn't hearit, I said.Play it again, louder this time.

They did.

Still nothing.Afew lights came on, but from her neighbors.

I was very disappointed.I expected some response. A rose. Akiss from the balcony. Even a tossed potted plant...Anything...

Since I paid for an hour I had the musicians play that same song over and over again.

Bob: Like in Casablanca, play it again Sam.

Willie: Yeah, Bob. The neighbors were all screaming from their open windows.

"Play something else!"

We continued lapping up the beer, three sheets to the wind by now.

The musicians were hoarse singing that same ballad over and over.They were glad when the hour was up.

We got into the taxis and left, a barrage of curses from the neighbors trailing after us.

Bob: What happened with Maria?

Willie: She just laid in bed, listeniing. I didn't know that in Mexico they don't come to the windowlike in those romanticRomeo, Juliet, June, moon, spoon stories.

Bob: I don't think she was too pleased, Willie, she must have been fuming.

Willie: Maybe so, Bob but fortified with all that beer I was feeling no pain. The next day I went to her home. Her Father opened the door

"You made us the biggest scandal in Chihuahua.There's a bus leaving at two.YOU be on it!"

He closed the door.

Bob: Did you take the bus?

Willie: Hell, yes! Ileft in a cloud of bus dust!

Bob: So you patched up your broken heart with duct tape and went on to hunt some new game, right? Bring your guitar, Willie, and play that song for me: I'm anxious to hear it

Willie: OK , Bob but for you I'll only play it once.

Bob: Once will be enough ,Willie, I don't understand Spanish words

They both laughed

A REDHEAD STORY

On the very first day of every elementary school year, teachers look their new charges over to see which ones have red hair. Then they tell them,"You're not going to give me any trouble this year, are you?

    The following red head story is a bit different. It begins in Bob's Bar..........

Bob: Danny, meet Bridie, the prettiest red-headed colleen from Cork County, Ireland. She just arrived from across the pond.

Danny: Slante, lass! You are an Irish beauty and that's no blarney! Do you dye that flaming red hair?

Bridie: No Danny boy, that's my natural color.

Danny: Reminds me of a red haired girl with red as bright as yours; care to hear about her?

Bridie and Bob: Tell us Danny.

Danny: She was only three, the only redhead of eleven kids. They had big families years ago. It was a Russian family of immigrants who spoke Little English. They told her she came from "korovu dupu" the cow's ass, her being the only one with red hair.

    When I saw her playing outside I always asked her in her language (I speak it too) OT DEH TI PRISLA? From where did you come? And she would always answer in her childhood innocence,

    "OT KOROVU DUPU"

Bridie and Bob: That's funny, Danny.

Danny: Wait, that's not the end.

Both: There's more?

Danny: Yes. Twenty years later, I was walking with my buddy down the street Where the family lived and who should be coming towards us pushing a baby carriage with her husband alongside and a little son in tow but her! The flaming red hair was unmistakeable.

She came abreast us, saw me, and stopped.

"OT DEH TI PRISLA?"

"OT KOROVU DUPU"

We both roared with laughter and hugged each other for a long time.

Finally we cleared the confusion for her husband and my buddy by telling them .They were amazed that we both remembered after all those years.

Bridie: I come from a large family too, Danny and Bob. Now I can tell everyone I came from the cow's ass.

Bob and Danny in unison: MOOOOOOOOOO!

THANKS(for)GIVING(me a)TURKEY

Gene: Hiya, Bob, beer me up!

Bob: Glad to, Gene. How was your Thanksgiving yesterday?

Gene; Fine, Bob. The chicken was excellent. Y'know my folks raise chickens.

Bob: No traditional turkey?

Gene: Sometimes Bob, but they're not hung up on trdition. When you raise chickens, you eat chicken. I was invited to a turkey dinner but turned it down, even after I supplied the turkey.

Bob: Now you have me confused, Gene.

Gene: Here's the story, Bob. The Sunday before the holiday I went with my family to our Russian church in S.Jersey. The mass in Russian is always unGodly long, pun in tended so I linger outside and socialize with old friends. One fellow, George, whom I hadn't seen in ages asked me about my whereabouts. I told him I was now living in N.Jersey punching a register at the Food Fair grocery chain. He in turn told me he was married, three kids, and working at the smelting plant in town

A day before Thanksgiving, who appears at my register with a huge turkey and a few cans of frozen juices but George. He was wearing a bright red hunting jacket Very conspicuos, standing out like a dirty fingernail in third grade.

Bob: He drove all that distance to buy a turkey?

Gene: Not George. Not him. He wanted a freebie. As my former Jewish landlady Mollie used to say about stingy guys like him." They are so tight they vodent pay ah nikel to see the Statue of Liberty take a s----. Another of her gems was,"They vod

-steal your eyes out if you werent looking" But enough of Mollie. Back to my story.

Bob: Yeah, go on, Gene.

Gene: So stupid me , I just rang up the juices for $1.50 pushed the turkey into two bags

He paid, gave me a bodacious grin and left. But that's not the end, Bob.

Bob: No?

Gene: Ten minutes later just enough time to go to his car and back, he's at my

register again with a bigger bird! What could I do? I rang up some small stuff he had

And waited for him to pay. He fumbled through his pockets looking for money.

Customers behind him were getting impatient and curious. Sweat was forming on

my forehead. Food Fair doesn't just fire you for stealing, they prosecute.

Finally he reached in his shirt pocket."Oh, here's a five dollar bill I

forgot about", he said.

Rapidly I gave him change and he left with another bird.

Thanksgiving Day at the table enjoying the chicken dinner with my family

the telephone rings.

It was George. He was inviting me for Thanksgiving dinner to gab, gobble, and git.

Bob: That's Chuzpah! Nerve!

Gene: I told him not to come to my store and slammed the phone down.

When I went back to work the boss called me into the office. He said he was watching me

the past week. Oh. Oh, I saw bars in front of me.

He offered me ass't mgr position since Sandra was leaving to have a baby.

I asked if it meant that I would have to work like her every Saturday night until

mid-night and beyond. When he said "Yes" I turned it down. Being single Saturday

Night was my night to howl. He told me to stay in the food line because people always have to eat and there will always be a job.

Bob: My weakness is lobsters, Gene, do you sell them ther? If so, I'd like to pay you a visit.

Gene: No, Bob, you're outa luck Incidentally the food fair went into chapter 11.

Bob: Probably too many free turkeys, Gene.

Gene: Quote the Raven,"Nevermore"

Bob: Good quote, Gene, fits the "fowl" experience you had.

Gene: Groan! For that you should be PUNished ,Bob.

Both laugh.

Now who does a bartender tell <u>HIS troubles to ??????</u>

Good question ! Ambrose Bierce's definition of happiness as being the agreeable sensation arising from another person's misery fits in here. Bartender Bob's troubles seem minor compared to the ones he has heard over the 30 years he tended bar from Las Vegas to North Carolina, but they didn't make him any more happier.

Surely you readers have a lot more interesting stories to tell than are in this book. Let's here them! Send them to abook6@yahoo.com and if they're in the next sequel coming soon you'll get a fat monetary tip and a free drink on the house.

Follow the Biblical injunction written somewhers in the Good Book that advises you to "Eat to the point of dullness and drink to elevation"

                Your "Spiritual" sympathizer,

                    Bartender Bob

HOLD THE PRESS ! Last minute submission by Jason- Thanks Jason!

Enjoy the dough and drink on the house!

XXX Kisses sweeter than wine ??

Bob: Welcome Jason and Greg; How did it go last night?

Greg: Let's talk about the weather, Bob.

Bob: Why, what's wrong, Greg?

Jason: Ha! Ha! He doesn't want to talk about it but I'll tell the world !

　　　I can't stop laughing...

Greg: Shut up. Jason!

Jason: Here goes anyhow, Bob. Remember the two beautiful twins Sheila and Sally

　　　We were drinking with last night?

Bob: Yeah, they were really downing the drinks but after all, you two were buying.

Jason: They both worked in the pocetbook factory for slave wages. Us ironworkers

　　　Make out like bandits but it's dangerous work and has a premium on youth.

　　　When we left they were a bit unsteady walking to the car. Greg got in the back seat with

　　　Sally and Sheila sat in the front with me. We pulled out and a minute later Sally

　　　Yelled, "Stop the car!"

Bob: Why?

Jason: It puzzled me too. So I pulled over to the side of the road and stopped. Sally got out

　　　Bent over and heaved her cookies all over the road. This was immediately after

　　　Greg kissed her.

It was a case of reverse esophageal peristalsis.

Greg: She was drunk,Bob and Jason stop using those big words just because You have a GED diploma!

Jason: From now on Greg, you're "Volcano Lips", a kiss from you makes a girl "erupt" all over the place.

Greg: You should talk, Jason, when you pucker up your lips look like a chicken's ass.

Bob: Fight nice fellows, look who's here, your last night companions!

The two girls sheepishly approach the boys at the bar. They profusely apologize for their over indulgence and promise moderation. Bob pours Four drinks and leaves to wait on other patrons.

Sally:Greg, it was that spicy Mexican meal I ate before we came to the bar.It backed up on me, I'm sorry.

Bob returns to the scene and hears Sally's explanation.

I must say you make a fine foursome.

Greg: You know the meaning of the word, Bob?

Bob: Yes, but let's hear yours.

Greg: You wine 'em, dine 'em, ask 'em. If they refuse you force 'em.

Jason: But never, never let Greg kiss 'em!

Greg: I'll never live that down.Down the hatch! Cheers!

All in unison-CHEERS!

TAXI! TAXI!

It's a quiet afternoon. Bob is behind the bar getting ready for the night's business. So far only one patron is at the bar nursing a beer. It's John, a regular. Most bars exist on those steady characters who support the bar business every day. The swinging doors open and Harry the Hack walks in. He greets John and orders a beer from Bob.

Bob: You're early Harry, no business?

Harry: Not much, Bob. After today I'm thinking of packing it in and getting a steady job with a steady income like John the postman here.

John: Yeah, I got tied of chasing rainbows. I don't get rich on this job, that's for sure but there's no heavy lifting, no poisons to breathe and walking keeps me in good shape plus I get benefits. But what happened today that put you over the edge, Harry?

Harry: Well, I was cruising the stem looking for a fare when Mike the Mall cop calls me over. Harry he says, take this woman to where she wants to go. I told the woman standing next to Mike to hop in the cab which she did. She gave me the address and we took off. It was in the ritzy section of town by the waterfront where all the swells live. She was well-dressed so I didn't expect much of a tip because I know how cheap these bums are especially docs and lawyers and fur-clad broads like this one. "Wait here, I'll be right back" she said and went up to the big mansion on the hill.

I waited.And waited.And waited.Time went by.

John and Bob: What did you do Harry?

Harry: I went to the mansion.Rang the bell.No one came so I went to the back.I saw an open gate and it dawned on me that she stiffed me on the fare! I was boiling mad!

Bob: Who wouldn't be.

John: What did you do then,Harry?

Harry: I went back to my cab thinking maybe she left something behind as sometimes people do.I opened the door and sure enough she did.

Bob: What was it?

Harry: A filthy pair of panties and she took a crap on the back seat! Boy,I was livid! I drove back to the Mall and saw Mike the cop.I told him how she screwed me out of the fare and the presents she left for me on the back seat of my cab.

Bob: What did Mike say,Harry?

Harry: He said,"Harry,if she doesn't claim them in thirty day they're yours.That's the law."

HAPPY BIRTHDAY!!

Bob: Well,well,well! The story of the two holes in the ground! Well, look who's here! The parched pedagogue of apathetic pupils!

Rudy: Enough of the alliteration;beam me up Bob with beer. Now we're even.

Bob: Ha! Anyhow what's new with the little midgets?

Rudy: Today we had a birthday party for George,the kid who always acts up in class.You know I have a routine we follow for birthdays.The kids recite a poem and sing happy birthday.The child makes a wish and blows out the candle on the Twinkie.Then he/she eats it.The Twinkie.

Bob: Sounds like a fine routine,Rudy, what's the poem?

Rudy: Count your garden by the flowers, never by the leaves that fall.Count your days by golden hours,don't remember clouds at all, Count your nights by stars, not shadows. Count your life by smiles, not tears, And with joy on every birthday, count your age by friends- not years.

Bob:Copy that for me Rudy,I'd like to have that.

Rudy:After George made his wish and blew out the candle, he turned to look at me and said,
"You're still here"
The class laughed.I did too.

A PARTING POEM

I wish these stories I could give,
To you without a charge,
Unfortunately I too must live,
And debts I must discharge.
If you beg, borrow, or steal this book,
Read it-----and I hope you'll find,
A word of cheer, a smile, a tear,
Or a passage you'll commit to mind.
Maybe a single line to quote,
Maybe a story to read again,
Then I will never think I wrote,
This book of tales in vain.

                        Evan Book - AKA - Bartender Bob

EPILOGUE

...at past three in the morning the place is quiet; the last drink served, the last man leaving, and one by one the lights are turned off.

The sounds linger, the talk and shouts, sighs and guffaws, and calls for "one more here." Then all fade into the dark.

Bartender Bob steps out into the near dawn night, a short walk to the end of the block on swollen feet and home. And the interlude of sleep until the next night.

Made in the USA
Charleston, SC
19 October 2013